For the Record: Confessions of a Vinyl-Soundtrack Junkie

Also by Bruce K. Hanson
The Peter Pan Chronicles
Peter Pan on Stage and Screen: 1904-2010

For the Record: Confessions of a Vinyl-Soundtrack Junkie

Bruce K. Hanson

Frontispiece: Carleton Carpenter and Joan Evans listening to "Aba Daba Honeymoon" from the MGM album of *Two Weeks with Love* in 1950. The record was the first soundtrack recording to become a top-of-the-chart gold record.

Front Cover Photo: Judy Garland listening to records in 1938.
Back Cover Photo: *White Christmas*, Decca ED 819

ISBN: 1534997067
ISBN 13: 9781534997066

Dedicated to Suzi Williams

Preface

EVEN AS A CHILD I was already a record geek. I would spend joyful afternoons listening to music while studying the album covers and reading the liner notes. In the early 1960s I noticed a discrepancy between what was playing on my vinyl and how it was credited in the liner notes. The MGM album was called *Something Wonderful* by Jane Powell. One of the songs, "We Never Talk Much," was a duet performed by a man and a voice other than Powell's. Another song, "Paris," just featured the man's voice! There was no mention of any other singers on the cover. The liner notes complimented Jane Powell's beautiful voice. How could this be?

A few years later I discovered that the uncredited voices belonged to Fernando Lamas and Danielle Darrieux and the songs were from a 1951 Jane Powell film, *Rich, Young and Pretty*. I understand how Jane's voice could have been confused with Danielle's in the duet with Fernando but how could they have mistaken Fernando for Jane on "Paris?" Apparently the record producer, the engineer and the designer never listened to the recording that was chosen. It gets worse though: the album was reissued a few years later on MGM's Lion label with the same blunders. It was not until MGM re-released their soundtracks in the 1970s that the inaccuracies were corrected and Jane Powell's version of "Paris" was released for the first time with the other songs from the film.

It is my hope that this book is void of any inconsistencies regarding the records discussed. However, if there are slip-ups, I know that some well-meaning collector of vinyl will let me know. All of the photographs, posters and album covers are from my collection. My family and friends have been very helpful in their assurances of the accuracy of my memories and how I have translated them to paper. In particular, I must thank Suzi Williams for sitting through my readings of these essays during late evening discussions. I am also grateful to her for making her house my home away from home while teaching in Norfolk, Virginia. During our annual summer vacations in Chincoteague, my partner Dale and my friend (and former student) Adam Pivirotto were also subjected to helping me select which essays would eventually end up in your hands via late night readings at the Anderton Cottage. Thank you, guys. A great debt to Lisa Ward, my friend and colleague, who edited the final draft for consistency in narrative style and grammar. Terese Toth lent me her scanner for several months and I am very appreciative. The folks at CreateSpace were very helpful and in particular I wish to acknowledge one of my editors, Laurel, for her excellent suggestions and corrections. Scott Brogan, founder and webmaster of The Judy Room, answered queries about recordings by Judy Garland. My friend Richard Tay of Sepia Records paved the way for this book when he asked me to write liner notes for various CDs he has produced over the years. That was a dream come true.

I am forever grateful to the songwriters, composers, singers, actors, and musicians of film and show music who have enriched my life. There's also the producers, musical directors, orchestrators, arrangers, sound engineers, and designers, who transformed that music to vinyl and CDs.

Finally, I must thank my partner Dale Neighbors who always supports my work in a myriad of ways. How quickly and extraordinarily the last eighteen years have passed since we first met. Here's to the next eighteen and more! "Wouldn't It Be Loverly?"

Table of Contents

Introduction

I SLICE THE TIGHTLY SEALED plastic, being careful not to hurt the jacket. Slowly pulling out the paper sleeve, I remove the gleaming black vinyl by holding the edges with my fingers, avoiding touching the surface at all costs as I carefully examine it to see if the record is indeed truly mint. These days there are sellers who reseal records to sell them as new-old stock. Usually, I go near the light beaming in from a window where I can see any flaws in the vinyl. Next, placing the record in a horizontal position, I balance it in the air and support it with my fingers directly on the record label to see if it is even slightly warped. So far, so good.

Lifting the hinged dust cover of my Dual turntable, I check that the proper stylus is in place, fit the record on the platter, gently place the tonearm over the beginning of the first selection on side one, and wait a few seconds for the needle to softly drop into the groove. The first contact between the needle and vinyl brings an indefinable joy, a myriad of dulcet sounds that might include a soft click, faint static, or a muffled, scratchy noise. Perhaps there may be nothing at all, but it is a warm kind of nothing. Then I sit and close my eyes or read the liner notes on the album cover as I take in the crisp, clear sounds of my favorite new recording.

These days it is difficult to buy a sealed soundtrack record from the golden age of the Hollywood musical or to find a mint copy of a classic Broadway musical in its first pressing. Of course there are reissues with added reverb (echo) for simulated stereo, but I prefer the flat sound of the original releases. And, of course, the original artwork.

Debbie Reynolds listening to MGM records in a publicity
photo for *Give a Girl a Break* from 1953.

I am a soundtrack junkie. I am not sure why, but at least I am not alone. Odds are that you who are reading this book are addicted to some genre of music on some level. When I say "soundtrack," I am referring not only to music recorded directly for movie musicals or as background themes for straight films but also to Broadway cast albums, pop music, and light jazz. What is it about musical comedy on vinyl that I can't resist? What is it that has me hooked on musicals? Why am I addicted to records?

In my art classes, my young students will paint or draw while listening to music on their iPods, tablets, or smartphones, sharing a set of earphones with a friend. When I was a theater student in college, friends would gather around to listen to the latest Broadway recording or to discover a treasure recently reissued. I still remember the sheer joy we experienced of Nancy Walker singing "I Can Cook Too" from the 1960 recording *On the Town*. Sharing music is a fundamental part of life—like storytelling. But as a fan of musical comedies, I can tell you the experience is more involved. There is an implied narrative even if you cannot read the libretto or see the play or film. There is a love story.

When I was younger, I always wanted to be that cute fellow courting a beautiful girl through song and dance. How safe it all was. How lovely to be able to convey romance without sex, that two people could love each other to such a degree that they could make love by singing and dancing without ending up in bed together. It was not until much later that I realized that I not only wanted to be the fellow who woos the girl with music, but that even more, I wanted to be the one wooed.

During my high school years in the early 1970s, Mom forced me to wear bell bottoms in her desperate attempt to make me stylish. I preferred straight-leg jeans, penny loafers, a light-blue oxford button-down collared shirt with only the top button open, and a beige-and-yellow-plaid hunter's jacket. That's what Wendell Burton wore in *The Sterile Cuckoo*. You remember him. He's the cute, dirty-blond-haired college student who spends much of the film trying to ditch Liza Minnelli. That's who I wanted to look like. No, not Liza, silly! Wendell. In fact, that's who I wanted. Wendell! Sadly, I was the victim of a flamboyant fashion period although I preferred a more conservative look.

My compromised attire hid my true identity. Even worse, I had to hide my feelings toward boys. Thus, music became a refuge quite early in my life, particularly soundtracks and Broadway cast record albums.

The first record albums that I can remember receiving as a child were the soundtrack of the Disney film *Peter Pan*; an Andy Williams album, *Moon River*; and a Topps record of *My Fair Lady* featuring Lola Fisher as Eliza Doolittle. As you can see, each was a soundtrack, a Broadway album of sorts, or a collection of film songs. Thus, I must thank Mom and later, my stepfather, Allen, for contributing to my musical comedy awareness at such an early age, for in essence, their gifts of such records as *Bye Bye Birdie, Carousel, The King and I*, and *Judy Garland at Carnegie Hall* marked the beginning of my addiction. I still own those records, not just because they are show tunes, not just because I like them, but because my parents gave them to me. And today, they still allow me to escape from a world of prejudice, hypocritical politics, violence, and crudeness. I don't smoke, and I don't drink. I guess being a soundtrack junkie is not such a horrible alternative. My desire to collect all vinyl releases of favorite titles is the appeal of album art and graphics, tactility, and a sense of preserving an aspect of the history of recorded music.

In the chapters that follow I will attempt to reevaluate key musical soundtracks of my life—in mono, stereo, simulated stereo, film and television soundtracks, original Broadway and Off-Broadway recordings, Technicolor, black and white, Dolby, Surround Sound, and even 3-D—as I examine my life as a soundtrack junkie. It's all for the record.

Doris Day listening to records for publicity for Warner Bros.

CHAPTER 1

Kiss Me Kate

Is it Tom, Dick or Harry?
Call me Tom, Harry or Dick

—COLE PORTER

THE FIRST SIGNS OF BECOMING a serious soundtrack addict occurred in 1966 at the age of twelve when I sold my comic book collection of *Superman, Detective, Batman, Adventure, The Fantastic Four,* and others for a grand sum of $200. Today, these same comics, some going back to 1939, would sell for a much bigger profit than my entire record collection, but records have given me more pleasure for a longer period. Instead of bringing the cash home or telling my parents about the sale and depositing it in the bank for college, which they undoubtedly would have forced me to do, I immediately went to Manhattan to spend half the money at Dayton's, a record store that specialized in rare albums. There were many such shops in the city then; amid the art galleries, boutiques, head shops, adult bookstores, and Orange Julius stands, there were several favorites—two Dayton's Record Shops in the Village, Colony Records, which was uptown on Broadway, and a shop in the mid-forties on the West Side. I remember that singer Tiny Tim used to shop at the latter to get ideas for songs he himself would record. The store specialized in out-of-print records of all formats—78s, 45 EPs, and ten- and twelve-inch 331/3 LPs.

Okay, wait a second! What are 78s, 45s, and 331/3s, you ask? In a nutshell, 78 rpm (revolutions per minute) records, along with Thomas Edison's cylinders, were the earliest form of commercial recordings for the public. At first they were one-sided platters of shellac, twelve-inch and ten-inch. There were also seven- and five-inch records for the kiddies. Then, both sides of the records contained recordings in a format sustained until the mid-fifties. Even longer lasting though, was, and is, what's called a "record album," which was essentially designed like a photo album: several sleeves, each containing one record sandwiched in a folder made of two illustrated cardboard covers.

In the late forties, RCA introduced a new format, the seven-inch 45 rpm record, which was lighter, easier to store, and unbreakable. If you are not from that era, they are those small records with the big holes you'll find aplenty at flea markets and even antiques stores. Initially, like their 78 rpm ten-inch counterpart, each side contained less than three minutes, but in a short period of time, the EP or extended-play 45 was introduced, which could contain up to seven minutes' worth of music. RCA began issuing 45 rpm record sets of Broadway shows while Columbia Records was pushing their new format, the LP, a long-playing record that contained much more music, because it ran at 331/3 rpm. At first these LPs were ten-inch so that they could fit in record dealers' ten-inch shelves, but soon the twelve-inch LP was being sold as well. Much of this had to do with Edward Wallerstein, Columbia's president, who believed that the listener should be able to hear an entire movement of a symphony on one side of an album. Ironically, in the seventies the eight-track cartridge, a tape made up of four double tracks for stereo, worked against this concept, interrupting a musical selection or movement to automatically change tracks.

Typically, a ten-inch LP could hold four songs per side, and the twelve-inch housed six. The first original Broadway cast album released on the twelve-inch format was *Kiss Me Kate* in 1948. A year later, Columbia Records recorded the Broadway cast of *South Pacific* twice—on metal master discs and on tape—although the master tapes were not used until the show music was released on CD in the 1990s. Interestingly, Bing Crosby was a major pusher of magnetic recordings, introducing the format via Ampex during the 1940s for prerecording his radio shows instead of broadcasting them "live."

The day I rode home on the Brooklyn BMT after selling my comic collection, I was carrying sealed soundtracks of the 1956 release of MGM's *The Wizard of Oz*, *The Unsinkable Molly Brown*, and *Kiss Me, Kate*. Oh yes, there was one other record that really doesn't belong in the same league as the others: the Decca Records soundtrack of *Flower Drum Song*. My younger brother, Mark, and I were exposed to this mediocre Ross Hunter/Universal Pictures' version of Rodgers and Hammerstein's Broadway musical as youngsters in 1966 when we were campers at Camp Moonbeam in Putnam Valley, New York. Although neither of us was particularly crazy about the film itself—indeed, Mark was generally not a musical film fan to begin with—it was one of his favorite record albums, though western tunes were more to his appetite. Almost every night, as we tried to go to sleep at our parents' absurdly appointed hour of eight o'clock, which was enforced throughout most of junior high school, we would put a stack of eight LPs on our record changer and then spend several hours listening to the music that was supposed to put us to sleep. We bargained and argued about which records we would listen to, because we each had only two dozen or so to begin with, but Mark always insisted on including *Flower Drum Song*. Even today, I find the overture thrilling—a prelude of wonderful things to come—even though the rest of the film is long, labored, and boring.

I had seen *The Wizard of Oz* several times during its annual CBS television broadcasts and even watched Debbie Reynolds kick up a storm as Molly Brown in a movie house in Hallock, Minnesota.

Kiss Me Kate was another story though; it had been one of my biological father's favorite films. I don't have many nice things to say about Vernon, because my earliest memory of him is that of fear. One night, several years before my shopping spree, while Vernon and Mom were still together, I was called into their bedroom in our simple ranch-style house in Comstock, Michigan. Cautious at first, since usually when one of us was called to their bedroom, it meant a spanking, I was surprised to see my father smiling and pointing to the television. "I thought you might wanna see this," he said as I approached him guardedly. "That gal can sure dance!" he declared. I looked at my father and then, feeling safe, turned my eyes to the small black-and-white television.

It was then and there that I first witnessed the talents of Ann Miller, who was singing and dancing "Tom, Dick or Harry" from *Kiss Me Kate*. I was immediately struck by her lusty yet humorous approach to the song, along with the terpsichorean talents of Bobby Van, Tommy Rall, Bob Fosse, and Carol Haney. More importantly, I sensed something special in what I would later come to recognize as the MGM look and sound.

The original 1953 soundtrack of the only 3-D
musical, *Kiss Me Kate*. MGM E 3077

A few years later, happily living in New York City with my mother, my brothers, and my stepfather, Allen, I discovered that indeed MGM released many soundtracks on vinyl. The day I came home with my "loot" from the sale of my comics, I opened the plastic wrappers that the records were sealed in, handling each record carefully by the edges so that my fingers would not leave their prints on the record surface, which, because of the oil residue, could collect dust (a record's worst enemy). I played each one over and over again—thrilled that *The Wizard of Oz* soundtrack included bits of dialogue (although it omitted "The Merry Old Land of Oz," which was listed on the record label); excited to hear Debbie Reynolds and Harve Presnell sounding as vibrant as they did in the movie theater and to know I would not have to endure another screening of *Flower Drum Song* to appreciate its music. What about *Kiss Me Kate*? Much to my chagrin, "Tom, Dick or Harry" was not included on the Metro album. Metro Records was a subsidiary of MGM Records, which I later learned often reissued abbreviated (*translation: cheaper*) versions of the original MGM releases. It would be another three years before I could find the complete out-of-print soundtrack. Where? Dayton's, of course! But by then, I was a full-fledged junkie, indulging a lifelong journey as a soundtrack addict.

CHAPTER 2

The Wizard of Oz

Someday I'll wish upon a star
And wake up where the clouds are far behind me

—HAROLD ARLEN AND "YIP" HARBURG

IT'S FUNNY HOW SOMETHING THAT might have embarrassed us in our youth later appears harmless and perhaps even poignant. When I was a child, there were only a few constants that I could count on: my brothers and the annual showing of *The Wizard of Oz*.

During my parents' separation, my father was supposed to take my brothers and me to Comstock, Michigan, from Brooklyn, New York, to empty our house and then get us back to my mother before school started. However, Vernon had other plans; he kept us in Comstock and reenrolled us in our old school. Then, about two months later, he unceremoniously dumped us off in Hallock, Minnesota, first at his mother's home and then with his sister, my aunt Joyce, who had five kids of her own to worry about.

Aunt Joyce and her family were quite welcoming, and I will always be grateful for their generosity. Yet, quite understandably, I missed my mother, whom I would not see for another year. Everything was different in that small town of Hallock. At the time there was one elementary school, a high school, an ice cream shop open only in the summer and run by the cafeteria ladies during their vacation from school, a bar, a supermarket, a cemetery, and a movie theater. Because it was such a small town, it was inevitable that I would learn stories about the family, which at first were dismissed as urban legend. My friends deemed one tale, of my great-aunts freezing to death during a fierce winter storm, the invention of "auntie-freeze." Another story had a great-uncle burn from the inside out when he accidentally drank acid, which was in a glass in a kitchen. Sadly, both stories were later revealed to be true!

The 1940 cast album of *The Wizard of Oz* features Judy Garland singing "Over the Rainbow" and "The Jitterbug." The Ken Darby Singers re-enacted musical sequences from the film on the remaining three 78 rpm records. Decca Album 74

During the separation from my parents, I was skipped a grade, which made me feel even more vulnerable in my new school. Then my older brother was sent to live with relatives in Minneapolis, leaving me with no champion to protect me. Sports were not my thing, so it was difficult to make friends, but fortunately, I was surrounded by my cousins Cathy, Beverly, Becky, Sonny, and Timmy at Aunt Joyce's, and in school we were joined by Cheryl and Susan, my other cousins who lived on a nearby farm. One or two kids in my sixth-grade class constantly teased me, but at Joyce's I was overshadowed by Timmy, who was much more "gay" acting than I was. Yet—and this still amazes me—no one in the house teased him for his feminine traits. He was just Timmy.

My aunt and uncle usually frequented the bar on Saturday nights, leaving my cousins, my younger brother Mark and me alone in the house. Because Becky was fifteen, she was given the responsibility to watch over us and make sure we did not get into too much trouble. Becky could be quite mean to us sometimes, but she liked me because I would sing "Downtown" to her friends on the telephone. I had a nice singing voice and was actually complimented by Becky and my cousins for my rendition of that particular song. In addition, although I didn't own the soundtrack album at this point, I knew practically all of the dialogue and songs from *The Wizard of Oz* by heart from its yearly telecasts and would often act out all the parts.

Somehow, my sixth-grade teacher got wind of my particular talents and asked me to perform *The Wizard of Oz* for the class. There I was skipping around the classroom as Dorothy, screeching at the top of my lungs as the Wicked Witch of the West, marching around as the Munchkins, flailing my arms hysterically as the flying monkeys, and singing "Over the Rainbow" while sitting on the teacher's desk with my legs dangling. I must have been quite the sight. Yet no one made fun of me. In fact, I received spontaneous applause at the end of each musical number and a roar of approval at the end of my performance. To top it off, the other sixth-grade teacher heard about my antics and asked my teacher if could perform the play for her class as well! Suddenly, no one was making fun of me anymore. Perhaps I was really good, or perhaps it was just that my classmates were amazed that I had the balls to sing and dance without any reservation; I am not sure, but I do know that from then on, I felt safe on the playground.

Movies were one of our favorite pastimes, and although there was only the one theater in Hallock, we saw almost a movie a week. In particular, I remember watching *The Unsinkable Molly Brown* and *What a Way to Go*.

The latter, with Shirley MacLaine, Dick Van Dyke, Paul Newman, Gene Kelly, Robert Mitchum, Bob Cummings, and Dean Martin was almost like a musical without songs in which a young woman finds herself widowed four or so times. As she recalls each marriage with her psychiatrist, it is shown as a series of flashbacks via various film genres such as silent film with Dick Van Dyke, Paul Newman in a foreign arts flick, Robert Mitchum in a glossy Ross Hunter picture, and Gene Kelly in a musical comedy. At the end of each film segment "The End" flashes across the screen. Mark and Sonny, thinking that the first "end" was the end of the entire movie, left the theater after only fifteen minutes.

In the summer, the family who owned the movie theater took an annual trip to California to choose the films for the upcoming year. When they came back, their home movies of Hollywood were projected in their theater before the featured film along with various trailers. Among the films scheduled for the year were *My Fair Lady* and *Mary Poppins*. However, I was not to see these musicals until many years later, because Mark and I left Hallock shortly after those projections. Perhaps that was better, as my appreciation for musicals increased with my maturity. I envy those who experience a great musical film that I have seen before for the first time. *The Wizard of Oz* is one of the handful of musicals that I can enjoy every year. I still remember Danny Kaye's introduction to the film, warning his young audiences that somewhere in the middle of the telecast, the film would change from black and white to color. "There's nothing wrong with your television sets," he added. "It's just the way the picture was made."

Years later, a friend of my partner's cried when she saw the film in color for the first time in a movie theater. As a child she had always waited for it to change to color, but her parents' television was a black-and-white model. I saw the film on the big screen at a special viewing for students at my college. Although I didn't shed any tears, I still found it a thrilling and memorable experience to finally see my favorite film blown up and in Technicolor.

CHAPTER 3

My Fair Lady

I think she's got it!
By George, she's got it!

—ALAN JAY LERNER AND FREDERICK LOEWE

SOMETIME IN THE EARLY 1960S, when I was seven or so years old, my mother bought me a record album called *My Fair Lady*. It wasn't the original Broadway cast recording; that was too expensive! Besides, I didn't even know what that was in those days. No, my album starred Lola Fisher, the understudy to Julie Andrews in the original Broadway run whom my mother had seen perform the role of Eliza Doolittle, singing the songs from the musical with Richard Torigi to the accompaniment of Al Goodman's Orchestra. I must have listened to that record, which I still own, hundreds of times. Despite the lack of liner notes or a synopsis of the play, I recognized that the songs belonged to some sort of a narrative, and though hummable, they were much more sophisticated than anything I had ever heard before. *What if...*thought my little seven-year-old brain. *What if they also put songs from movies on records too?* Although it would be a few years before I would buy my own records, my birthday and Christmas wish lists always included record albums. Some of the songs or albums that I received included the soundtrack from Disney's *Peter Pan*, Andy Williams singing *Moon River and Other Movie Hits*, the soundtrack from *The Music Man*, the *Mickey Mouse Club*, and a 45 rpm record of "Bye, Bye, I'm

Going Away" (whose lyric tickled me: "I'm never, never, never, never coming back; I loved you once but you're a bit too fat").

Lola Fisher, Julie Andrews's understudy for *My Fair Lady*, appeared on a recording whose album cover went through several incarnations and even appeared on other labels. Diplomat 2214

To know that there was a place in New York called Broadway where people paid to see plays with music was akin to knowing the location of the mythical Shangri-La—only Broadway was real! About a year after learning about the Great White Way, I was cast in my fourth-grade class's Christmas play (the title still escapes me), which essentially concerned a plot in which Santa Claus decides not to deliver presents that year. Mrs. Taylor, my teacher, worked with us to create a huge frame that would appear as a television while several of my classmates were assigned to the major roles of newscasters, Santa, Mrs. Claus, and his lead elf. My friend Jeffrey, a very good-looking boy who early on learned how to kiss up, played the elf, and I was given the role of the mailman who delivered mail to the network, since Santa was no longer accepting letters from children. My character appeared only twice, and rather briefly, in the forty-five-minute play with such mundane lines as "Well, here is the mail!" and "Got a big bundle here!" After my second scene, Mrs. Taylor directed me to leave the stage, making my total stage time less than one minute.

Studying the script at home, I noticed that there was nothing in the stage directions to indicate that the mailman should leave the stage after his second scene. Armed with my limited knowledge of the Broadway shows my parents had seen when they lived in New York City, the next day I asked Mrs. Taylor if I could talk to her privately before we began rehearsing. Apparently, I looked quite upset, because Mrs. Taylor asked me if everything was all right. "No," I answered quietly. "Everything is not all right."

"What's the matter?"

"Mrs. Taylor, my parents saw our play on Broadway, and they told me that the mailman never left the stage after his second entrance."

"Well," my teacher asked tentatively, "what would you suggest? The mailman has no more lines."

"My mother told me that he sat down at the side of the scene, where he watched and reacted with his face." Mrs. Taylor studied me carefully. *Does she know I'm lying, that my parents never saw the play on Broadway?* Then she smiled.

"All righty then! If that was good enough for Broadway, then it's good enough for us." Thus, from that rehearsal on and the one evening performance of the play, I sat on stage for almost half the play. After the show was over, parents lined up to congratulate Mrs. Taylor on her fine directing job. Hidden around the corner, I watched with trepidation as my parents approached my teacher. Although I couldn't hear any of the conversation, it looked cordial and polite, with all parties smiling. My parents walked away to the refreshment stand, Mrs. Taylor received compliments from another set of parents, and I knew that I was safe. Whew!

Many years later, at the age of nineteen, I was appearing in a children's play, *The Freelance Kid*, Off-Off Broadway at the 13th Street Repertory Theatre. The music was composed by David Friedman, whose credits include several

Tony-nominated musicals in addition to his conducting the music scores for Walt Disney's animated films *Beauty and the Beast, Aladdin, Pocahontas*, and *The Hunchback of Notre Dame*. Originally assigned as the understudy to all of the men's roles, the actor playing the Freelance Man suddenly gave notice, because he had been cast in the national touring company of *Grease*. In less than two weeks' time, I would be playing his part. David gave me a cassette tape to practice the title song, and the director was extremely patient with me as I tried desperately to convey a confident character.

The play opened on a Saturday matinee, and my mother and stepfather, Allen, were in the audience. After the performance I went home to their house on Staten Island for the weekend. During supper that night my mother pulled out a box of ephemera she had saved from my school days so she could insert the program. Leafing through the box I found the program from my fourth-grade Santa Claus play. I had long forgotten my clever ruse as I peered inside to find that the play had been written by Mrs. Taylor! *Holy shit!* I looked at my mother, who didn't notice my facial reaction to the content. "Do you remember this play?" I asked.

"Of course I remember," she replied. "You had only two lines. You've come a long way, Brucie." I studied her face as carefully as Mrs. Taylor had studied mine way back when. She didn't know. Definitely...maybe.

CHAPTER 4

Bye Bye Birdie

What's the story, morning glory? What's the word, humming bird?
Have you heard about Hugo and Kim?

— "The Telephone Hour," Lee Adams and Charles Strouse

When we weren't playing records, my friends and I were often playing pranks. By today's standards they were probably quite tame, but at the time, in the late sixties, we thought them clever and maybe even a little sophisticated.

Steven and I used to make prank calls from his parents' apartment on Avenue X in Brooklyn. The simplest I can remember is when Steven would arbitrarily pick out a number of an Italian deli from the telephone directory and dial. When the store owner answered, Steven would ask if his store carried Dr. Pepper in a bottle.

"Yes, of course we have Dr. Pepper in a bottle," was the usual answer.

"Well, let him out!" Steven would shout into the receiver, and then he'd hang up. Okay, not as clever as I remembered. What about this one:

We would call various numbers until a woman answered. As my voice had not yet changed, Steven would talk, saying that he was calling from Ma Bell's. He'd explain that the local telephone company was working on the lines and some of that work involved high-voltage equipment. He advised the lady of the house not to pick up the receiver during the next forty-five minutes under any circumstances, because a telephone repairman could be electrocuted.

Then, after securing assurances that she would, indeed, not answer the call, Steven would hang up. After a few minutes we would call back and let the phone ring a couple of times, then call again, only this time with four or five rings. We would call one last time and let it continue ringing until, finally fed up with the rings, the lady of the house would pick up the receiver. Then, at the top of my lungs, I would scream into the phone, hang up, and roll around Steven's living room floor in convulsions of laughter.

The Broadway cast recording of *Bye Bye Birdie*
with Chita Rivera, Dick Van Dyke, Paul Lynde,
and Susan Watson. Columbia KOL 5510

My friend John's pranks were "live action"; that is, not on the telephone but rather in person, so we could watch the reactions of our victims. My favorite abuse occurred at dusk. We would take thin blue thread and tie it back and forth from the telephone pole to his neighbor's front porch and then simply sit on his porch and watch as unsuspecting pedestrians walked through our spider web, flailing their arms helplessly, because the thread could hardly be seen. Our only task was to keep a straight face to convey innocence over the incident. Once, however, some tough Italian boys didn't think it was so funny. John was Italian too and I was Jewish but we were not tough. We barely made it inside John's house and locked the door.

These telephone pranks remind me of the "Telephone Hour" in *Bye Bye Birdie*. Each summer I was shipped away with my brother Mark to Camp Moonbeam in the Putnam Valley of New York. There, I was cast as Hugo Peabody in the camp production of *Bye Bye Birdie*. I loved rehearsing it, but, as with most plays at Moonbeam, for reasons unknown, there was never an actual performance. The following Christmas I asked my parents for the soundtrack and original cast recordings of that show as well as other Broadway shows, including *The King and I*, *Oklahoma*, and *Carousel*.

A few weeks before Christmas, Steven came over, and because my parents were not home, we began an extensive search to see if they had purchased the records yet. We located the albums at the top of their bedroom closet. A week later Steven was over for a meal and innocently blurted out that we had found the records. Well, needless to say, my parents were furious and threatened not only to take back the records but also not to buy me anything else for Christmas. I promised that I would never repeat such an act again, and after a few more days, all was forgotten and forgiven. Thank goodness! If they had carried out their threat and returned the records, they would not have been able to get their money back. You see, after Steven left my house the day we uncovered the albums, I could not control myself. I carefully sliced the seals of the plastic wrap on several of the records with a razor blade and listened to them on my record player in my bedroom—alone and quietly, the way addicts do.

CHAPTER 5

White Christmas

Love, you didn't do right by me
You planned a romance that just hadn't a chance and I'm through

—IRVING BERLIN

THE FIRST WOMAN I CAN ever remember being in love with was Rosemary Clooney. Although I was only eight years old when I first saw her on the big screen, in VistaVision, no less, it was almost a decade later before I bought one of her albums. There were three reasons for omitting her from my collection of records: one, I knew of her only from one Paramount film musical; two, Clooney records were not exactly popular in the late sixties and early seventies and therefore, not easy to come by; and three, my allowance would not allow the indulgence of buying one of her out-of-print albums. And the out-of-print album I most coveted was one that was never issued—the soundtrack to *White Christmas.*

Most of the rest of the cast of *White Christmas* were under contract to Decca Records, whereas Rosemary Clooney was part of the Columbia Records family. Therefore, Bing Crosby, Danny Kaye, Peggy Lee, and Trudy Stevens, who dubbed for Vera-Ellen, recorded the score, with Joseph Lilley conducting the film's original though truncated orchestrations, for a twelve-inch album, while Clooney made her own recordings that were gathered together on a ten-inch LP.

Rosemary Clooney wore this stunning gown designed by Edith Head for her performance of the ultimate torch song, "Love, You Didn't Do Right by Me," in Irving Berlin's *White Christmas*.

The soundtrack album of *White Christmas*—or perhaps I should say the perfect soundtrack album of *White Christmas*—remains an elusive recording for which I have searched high and low since my early childhood. Not quite a year old when the film was first released, I remember seeing a rerelease of it in a movie house in Kalamazoo, Michigan, when I was in the third grade. From the sumptuous opening credits, wrapped up like a beautiful Christmas present, and the lilting overture, the film remains a holiday treat. Incidentally, Bing Crosby delivers his best version of "White Christmas" at the beginning of the film to the accompaniment of a music box.

For a few years after the rerelease of *White Christmas*, it was broadcast on NBC's *Saturday Night at the Movies*, and it became a tradition for my brother Wayne and me to watch it while my parents were out. Each Christmas, starting with 1962 or so, I would look in the record departments of Topps and other stores to see if they sold the soundtrack album, but to no avail. Years later, when I was eleven and living in New York City, Nana, my grandmother, took us to Radio City Music Hall for their annual Christmas show and movie. Nana was already aware of my fondness for Rosie, because there was a huge photo of her pulled from an old *New York Daily News* hanging in my bedroom. "Why does he have a poster of Rosemary Clooney?" she asked my mother.

"Better her than a boy," Mom answered. Did she know something I didn't know?

While strolling along Seventh Avenue to Radio City, we stopped in a record shop that specialized in out-of-print records. Nana bought a rock 'n' roll record for Wayne while I browsed through their show section. Then, looking up at the records displayed on racks high around the store, I spotted a ten-inch album of *White Christmas* with all of the songs performed by Rosemary Clooney. I don't know where I got the nerve—perhaps I was in shock—but I begged Nana to buy it for me. She asked the old woman who ran the shop for its price. "Thirty dollars," she answered flatly, as if the sale didn't mean a thing.

Nana then asked if she could look at the album. The woman brought out a small stepladder, grabbed the record, and gave it to Nana, who quickly inspected it and returned it to the shopkeeper. "Nonsense—this record is used! And there's a small stain on the front cover. There's no way I am going to pay thirty dollars for a used record."

I was deflated.

The ten-inch *White Christmas* LP with Rosemary Clooney.
It was also released as a 78 rpm album, a two record 45 rpm
EP set, and as two separate EP records. Columbia CL 6338

Two years later, on November 13, 1966, I received a reel-to-reel tape recorder for my bar mitzvah, which I used during the Christmas season to tape the audio of the whole film of *White Christmas* from our television set. I know what you are thinking: *A Jewish boy lusting after a Christmas album?* We were reformed Jews who celebrated Christmas and Easter. Setting the microphone in front of the TV speakers, I begged everyone in my family not to make a sound during my recording session. I listened to that tape many times until I was in high school, when, one day, I passed that same Seventh Avenue record shop with my friends John and Philip. Although there was a scary-looking man with huge thick glasses working there, I asked him if he might have a copy of *White Christmas* with Rosemary Clooney. He replied that he did not think so, because he was sure they had sold their only copy. However, he called to someone in the back room, and out stepped the same old woman whom I had met there four years before. *She was still alive!* Unless Frankenstein had cloned her in his laboratory deep in the basement of the building. And in her hands was that same copy of *White Christmas* with the same stain on the cover. I could not contain my excitement, telling the woman I had wanted that very album since I was eleven years old. When I asked about the price, she laid her eyes upon me and then upon the album. "Forty dollars," she answered nonchalantly. Surely it should have gone down in price!

"Excuse me, but why has it gone up in price?" I asked. "A few years ago it was only thirty dollars."

"It's very rare," she responded without feeling. "It's a collector's item." Once again I walked out of the store empty handed.

A few more years had passed when, now in college with a part-time job, I once more marched into that store, saw the same album with the same stain, picked it up nonchalantly, asked the price, and heard the same old woman reply forty dollars. "I'll give you thirty!" I answered back with confidence. "This record has been in this store for at least ten years. You can see no one else wants it."

"It's forty dollars," she said sternly.

"Thirty-five, and not a penny more," I replied with equal determination.

"Forty dollars!" she barked back.

"It's a deal!" I opened my wallet to pay her. At last, the treasure was mine. As I removed forty dollars, she placed the record in a bag and loudly pronounced, "That will be forty-two dollars and eighty cents."

I looked up from my wallet.

"Tax!"

I shuffled through the papers in my wallet even though I was perfectly aware that all I had left was carfare for the train and ferry ride home from Manhattan to Staten Island. "I don't seem to have any more money," I admitted rather timidly. The woman was about to take the record out of the bag, but after a long look at me, she miraculously softened, took my forty dollars, and gave me the record. "You owe me two dollars and eighty cents!"

A week later I returned to pay the tax.

CHAPTER 6

Judy Garland at Carnegie Hall

Oh, do it again
I might say no, no, no, no, no, but do it again

—George Gershwin and Buddy DeSylva

When I was fourteen years old, I asked my parents if they would buy me the soundtrack album of *A Star Is Born* for Christmas along with the soundtrack to *High Society*. Although I had not yet seen *Star*, I had heard a recording of "Swanee" on the radio, and it was that particular song I so desperately wanted. My mom could not find the album because the Columbia record was out of print and their subsidiary, Harmony Records, was still a few years away from their own reissue.

You can imagine my initial disappointment on Christmas morning when I opened my gifts and found no *A Star Is Born*. But what was this? *High Society* and two other Judy Garland albums—both in mono sound—*The Best of Judy Garland* on Decca Records, which featured an array of songs from the late thirties to mid-forties that Judy recorded while under contract to MGM, and another album titled *Live at Carnegie Hall*. As I played the latter, I could not get over the excitement generated by the overture conducted by Mort Lindsey on that distant April 23, 1961, evening.

The audience was elated even before Judy's first vocal! By the end of that song, "When You're Smiling," I understood. I found myself in a state of bliss, as if I were actually in the audience. Then came "Almost Like Being in Love," "Do It Again," "San Francisco," "Rock-a-Bye Your Baby," and "Over the Rainbow." "Swanee" followed, but by that track I was hooked on *Carnegie Hall*. By the end of the day I had played "Swanee" several times for my family and my older brother's best friend, Artie, who told me that Garland was considered one of the best singers in the world. As a kid in the early seventies I would play the double album on my portable record player in my backyard as I set about doing such mundane chores as painting the deck or cleaning our above-ground pool. My cousins next door would watch me working and tease me about my music. When I was sixteen, I found the Harmony reissue of *A Star Is Born* at Korvettes on Staten Island.

Judy Garland at Carnegie Hall was released on all formats including this 45 rpm EP record. Capitol/EMI EAP 1569

By the mid-nineties my copy of *Carnegie Hall* was pretty much worn out, so I purchased a stereo Japanese reissue and gave away my original mono. Still later I bought the limited-edition black box Capitol album that was released with Capitol Vice President Alan W. Livingston's letter and an 8-by-10-inch glossy photo of Judy. In 2000 I hesitantly shelled out some forty bucks for the 24-karat-gold CD by DCC Compact Classics, the one that had "everything." I was overwhelmed, as if hearing the original album for the first time. Judy's voice was louder than her orchestra and closer to the listener. Apparently, the gold CD set sold out rather quickly and now commands several hundred dollars for a copy. Now, as I am writing this chapter, I am listening to *The Historic Concert Remastered* in mono sound from JSP Records. And still, I am thrilled at each listening. As a matter of fact, one afternoon after school, while I was writing a review for this latest incarnation, a group of custodians came to clean my art room and asked who that wonderful singer was. When they had completed their tasks and departed, one man remained to tell me that he loved Judy as well as her daughter Liza. He was so excited about the recording and open with his opinion that I could not refrain from asking, "Are you family?"

"Of course," he replied, "although I have to keep it on the down-low here." I got up from my chair and we hugged each other, and then, laughing and chatting a bit, we listened as Judy sang "San Francisco."

I find it amazing that *Judy at Carnegie Hall* has never gone out of print since its initial release. It was the number one LP for thirteen weeks and remained on the charts for an additional eighty-one weeks! It won five Grammy awards, including Best Female Vocalist, Album of the Year, and Best Album Cover. It has been issued on 45 rpm EP play, seven-inch 331/3 rpm for jukeboxes, reel-to-reel, cassette, eight-track, and CD. You can even download it. When first released on CD in 1987, it was abridged to fit one disc, but there was such a public outcry that Capitol Records responded in 1989 with the release of a two-disc version. Oddly, Capitols' new disc set replaced the "live" version of "Alone Together" with a studio version from Judy's *That's Entertainment* album. To the rescue came producer Andy Wiswell and Steve Hoffman, an audio engineer responsible for giving face-lifts to recordings when transferring them to CD, who searched and found the original backup tapes for *Carnegie Hall* in the Capitol vaults. The whole process reminds me of the song "Do It Again" that Judy so tenderly sang in the concert. My motto, which I share with my high school art and acting classes: "Do it again; do it better; do it best!"

Too often I have encountered students in my high school visual art classes who, after completing one drawing or painting assignment, say they are bored. "I've already done a drawing or painting," they whine. *Art is like sex: you don't stop after the first time and never do it again. No, you practice and practice until you get it right…and then practice some more to get it better. But… you should be married!*

Or, in my acting classes, filled with thirty-four to thirty-seven students each, a few students would squeal, "I know my lines! Why do I have to rehearse?"

Acting is like sex: You can do it alone, but it's better with two people! But… you should be married!

Anyone who has been directed by me remembers that even after giving what they think is their best rehearsal performance, I will yell out in my best Monty Python imitation, "Do it again!"

CHAPTER 7

The Harvey Girls

These little words I know can never show how true I'll be,
But if you don't believe me, just you wait and see.

—JOHNNY MERCER AND HARRY WARREN

MY UNCLE BERNARD ON LONG Island was at one time a record collector of sorts. Married to my mother's sister, Audrey, he was the complete opposite of his wife: she was high strung and high maintenance, and he was laid-back and, well, almost comatose in my young eyes. To be fair to my aunt, I believe that she probably suffered from an undiagnosed bipolar disorder. I hope that's the case, because at my mother's funeral, Wayne, my older brother, made a touching speech saying that my mother's family was beautiful and what a comedown it was when she married Vernon.

One of my cousins stepped toward me after Wayne's testimony and whispered, "Wayne is wrong! Your mother's [immediate] family was not beautiful. Her sister was a %&$#! And her father was a goddamn two-timing, lying bastard." Shocked as I was to hear this in front of Mom's coffin, I knew that many in the family felt the same about her father and sister. Yet, even after all the years of the abuse my mother suffered from her family, I feel compelled to share a sweet memory of Audrey.

During an illness that weakened my mother considerably, my father was having an affair with another woman while his young wife was bedridden upstairs. I was only nine at the time when I walked into our family room in the basement and saw them sitting very innocently on our couch. Too innocently, I thought. Perhaps I didn't know the actual word *affair*, but I knew that they were having one. The "other woman" was my father's secretary. How original was that? She too was married, with a small daughter of her own. In addition to my father, she stole my stuffed animal toy.

Zippy the Monkey was my favorite toy from the moment I discovered him under our Christmas tree at the age of three. I took him everywhere: to the park, on family outings, and on long trips. Unfortunately, on a visit to Long Island he accompanied me to Audrey and Bernard's pool club. Naturally, Zippy took a dip, causing his stuffing to condense and gather in his forearms and near the feet, his body thus resembling Popeye's. Although he looked pretty pathetic, Zippy remained by my side whenever possible. A year or so after Zippy's drowning, my father's "other woman" noticed his pathetic condition and suggested that she take him home to open him up and restuff him. Tentative about the whole operation to begin with, not to mention the idea of being separated from Zippy for the first time in our lives, I agreed, since she was a friend of Mom's and Vernon's secretary. At this point I had no idea about their relationship.

I never saw Zippy again. Vernon told me that he was given to the daughter of his playmate, and he tried to comfort me with words to the effect that I was a big boy now. At the time I didn't know any curse words but *hell,* but if I could have expressed myself openly without getting my ass whipped with a strap, I would have shouted, "WHAT THE FUCK?"

Meanwhile—and I found out this part only recently from Wayne—Mom came home from work one day to a letter similar to the one received in the title song from the film *Meet Me in St. Louis*:

When Louis came home to the flat
He hung up his coat and his hat
He gazed all around, but no wifey he found
So he said, "Where can Flossie be at?"

A note on the table he spied
He read it just once, then he cried
It ran, "Louie dear, it's too slow for me here
So I think I will go for a ride."

One of my favorite albums is this 1957 twofer which
includes the songs from the 1944 film *Meet Me in St.
Louis* and *The Harvey Girls* from 1946. Decca DL 8498

Vernon ran away with his secretary, and Mom immediately suffered a
complete breakdown. Within twenty-four hours, Aunt Audrey and her cousin
Harriet flew from New York to Kalamazoo, Michigan, to rescue us, literally.
They arrived early the next evening at our house with my mother's friends
from our synagogue and quickly packed us with a few belongings into two
cars along with my sick mother. We slept overnight on the floor at Mom's
friend's house, and the next morning we were all on a flight to New York City.
My younger brother, Mark, and I lived with Cousin Harriet and her family

while Wayne stayed with Audrey. Mom was admitted to a hospital, and Mark and I did not see her again for about four or five months.

While writing this chapter, Wayne told me that our dog, Clancy, who had been left with a neighbor, went wacko. I never knew that. Even more shattering was the new knowledge that Mom wanted Vernon back. There was a reconciliation during which Vernon once more betrayed her trust when he kidnapped us.

During the late sixties and early seventies, Mom and her new husband, my wonderful stepfather, Allen, would take us on annual pilgrimages to Long Island, fighting that awful holiday traffic, to celebrate Passover with Audrey, Bernard, and all of the cousins. During one visit, before the lengthy meal and reading of the Haggadah in Hebrew, I was looking through Bernard's records when I spied a copy of the 78 rpm record set *The Harvey Girls*, with Judy Garland. I owned an LP version that shared songs from *Meet Me in St. Louis*, but I had never seen a copy of the 78 set. I don't know where I got the chutz-pah, but I asked my uncle if I could have it, because I was now collecting 78s. Bernard replied, rightfully, that he too collected records and that he could not give it away. I was disappointed not only for myself but for the album, because my younger cousin, the son of Audrey and Bernard, was often destructive, and would surely eventually destroy the set in time. Right I was!

Each year we celebrated Passover at Audrey and Bernard's, I would open their record cabinet and witness the slow process of destruction forced upon *The Harvey Girls*. Five years later, while observing shivah for my grandfa-ther, that "goddamn two-timing, lying bastard" referred to earlier, I noticed that the set was completely destroyed, its records broken and the album cover ripped. By this time, I was in college and living in Manhattan and finally owned my own 78 rpm copy of *The Harvey Girls*.

Audrey passed away several years before we lost Mom, but she was no longer speaking with her despite Mom's attempts to be close with her only sister. In fact, Audrey was not speaking to most of her family. But she and Bernard remained together "till the end." For several years Audrey's Passover Seders were attended by almost everyone in the family. Recently my favorite cousin informed me that one year, Audrey invited Bernard's girlfriend and his girlfriend's husband to the Seder. And they both accepted the invitation! Armed with the knowledge that everyone in the family was aware that Bernard was having an affair, Audrey carried on admirably, serving dinner with her hired help while playing the role of gracious hostess. Poor Audrey; she suffered a lifetime with her own "goddamn two-timing, lying bastard" while Mom, after spending sixteen years with Vernon, her "goddamn two-timing, lying bastard," was happily married to Allen for another forty-nine years. My mother's name was Sonia, but everyone called her Sunny. As indeed she was. I hope that Aunt Audrey had sunny days too.

CHAPTER 8

The Singing Nun

I will tell of Dominique as I sing this little song
And when I sing the chorus all the world will sing along!

— Jeanne Deckers and Randy Sparks

The Singing Nun is one of those films that leaves the viewer with that oft-quoted phrase, "What were they thinking?" Debbie Reynolds as a nun who sings, plays the guitar, rides a scooter, and saves souls? Can it really be as bad as it sounds? The answer is a resounding yes!

A fictitious account of the success of Sister Souire's songs, the film tells of Sister Ann (Reynolds) who is starting her new assignment at a convent in Belgium. There, the unconventional sister meets up with such conventional characters as the bumbling Father Clementi played by Ricardo Montalbán, Greer Garson as the prioress, acting even more pompous than Peggy Wood's Mother Superior in *The Sound of Music*, and the antagonistic Sister Cluny portrayed in her usual over-the-top fashion by the glorious Agnes Morehead. Also included was Chad Everett as Sister Ann's former beau, Katherine Ross as the slutty sister of one of Sister Ann's students, and Ed Sullivan as, well, who else? Ed Sullivan! Sister Souire had performed some of her songs, including "Dominique" on Sullivan's show, creating an instant and huge demand from the public of her songs on records.

The Singing Nun MGM S1E-7 ST

Obviously the film was given the go-ahead on not only the strength of the billing of Debbie Reynolds, who had recently won accolades as well as an Academy Award nomination for best actress for her performance in the film version of *The Unsinkable Molly Brown,* but also the overwhelming success of Julie Andrews in *The Sound of Music.* Suddenly, musicals with nuns and bad humor were in. Yet, this film is so bad that it makes the television series of a few years later, *The Flying Nun,* a classic. I seem to remember from my youth that there was even one segment in that series that had Sister Bertrille as played by Sally Field, in her early post-*Gidget* phase, teaching her students how to sing a song in a fashion similar to Debbie Reynolds teaching her students to sing "A Pied Piper's Song," which in turn was a cheap rip-off of Julie Andrews teaching the von Trapp children "Do Re Mi." It's almost biblical as one iconic moment begets one poor carbon copy after another. Like the film that inspired it, *The Flying Nun* wasted the talents of another veteran actress, Madeline Sherwood. Hollywood was so transparent in those days. It still is.

So what then, is the saving grace (forgive the pun) of *The Singing Nun*? The original soundtrack album, silly. I received the LP as a birthday present from my parents when I was twelve. Even before I opened the plastic that sealed the gatefold cover, I was excited by the album cover art: an iconic image of Debbie Reynolds riding a scooter in full habit with a guitar slung over her shoulder as she waves to the viewer. Not a photo, mind you, but a painting that, with the album graphics, promised to be as exciting as MGM's greatest musicals, at least in the mind of this twelve-year-old. The real Singing Nun, Soeur Sourire, took the name of Jeanne Deckers (her birth name was Jeannine Deckers) after she gave up her vows and lived with another woman in the biblical sense. Deckers never saw a cent of the royalties from her songs as she signed all benefits to her convent. Ironically, in the 1970s she was sued by the Belgian government for back taxes and the convent disavowed any responsibilities. Deckers' real life was much more powerful drama than the screen treatment by MGM.

As with most of the soundtrack recordings I owned, I had not seen the film itself. This one still puzzles me, as I believe it opened at Radio City Music Hall for the Easter show, to which Nana surely would have taken us boys. In any case, *The Singing Nun* played an even bigger part in my young life, which I will get to shortly.

I was not disappointed when I played the album on my record player. No, it was not *The Sound of Music*, but it was a collection of lovely Christian-themed melodies with Debbie Reynolds at her unaffected best, singing simply and clearly, whether solo or in harmony with the "sisters," with guitar accompaniment or a full orchestra. Even the instrumental version of "Lovely" was, I hate to repeat it, lovely, and the finale, "Kyrie" from *Missa Luba*, was one of the most exciting chants I had ever heard. In a short time, *The Singing Nun* became my favorite record album, alongside *Fiddler on the Roof*.

During the next year, while attempting to bring up my grade in math (which eventually climbed from 55 percent to 80 percent in one semester; sorry, but I had to brag), I also was taking bar mitzvah lessons a few days a week after school. I was never so uncomfortable in my life, for, despite being born Jewish—and proud of it, like Anne Frank, whose diary I had recently read—my family were reformed Jews, not Orthodox. I was the dreamer in the family, the artist. Allen and my mother not only kept any judgments to themselves, but also openly encouraged my interest in art and theater, and my musical tastes. As Allen was also Jewish, my parents decided that the family would make great strides in keeping the faith. Mom would come home to our apartment in Brooklyn on Friday nights after a long day's work in Manhattan and make a full Sabbath meal, complete with homemade chicken soup, chicken, and all the trimmings. Thankfully, during the summers—this was the pre-air-conditioning period in our lives—they would stop the formalities and simply take us to Nathan's in Coney Island, where we would enjoy hot dogs, pineapple drinks, and a ride or two on the bumper cars. It was one of the best times to see Allen laugh, enjoying the rides perhaps even more than "his boys."

When I told my best friend, Steven Hitchcock, that I was going to ask my parents if I could play my favorite records at my bar mitzvah reception, he looked at me rather skeptically. "*The Singing Nun* too?"

"Of course," I replied. "My parents said it was going to be my day and I could have what I want." And I did. They didn't even flinch when I asked. In fact, if memory serves me, my mother made it sound like it was her idea that I include *The Singing Nun*, along with my other suggestions, the original cast recordings of *The King and I, Carousel*, and of course, *Fiddler on the Roof.*

The big day arrived with the inevitable fear of ruining the haftarah in front of my family and the whole congregation. Once past that ordeal, the reception—a modest but nonetheless grand celebration, at least in my mind—was held at Adams on the Park in the Yorkville section of Manhattan. All of my family was there, including Dada, my "goddamn two timing, lying bastard" grandfather, his ex-wife, Nana, and uncles, aunts, cousins, and best of all, my friends—Steven Hitchcock, John Pampinella, Patrick Moore, Susan Leftcovitz, and Glenn Sherman. During the proceedings, as I joined Allen and my mother in greeting our guests table by table, my music played from the portable record player hidden behind the table full of gifts. "Whistle a Happy Tune" was heard, and there wasn't a word from anyone. The song "If I Loved You" graced the air and still there was not a word. Then, Debbie Reynolds singing "Dominique." Still nothing!

A few months ago my cousin Bonnie reminisced about that recording, wondering why my mother never suspected that I was gay. "I never really knew at that age," I answered in defense of Mom.

"Well, the rest of us knew from the time you were five."

L. to R. My older brother, Wayne, younger brother, Mark, Mom, me, and my stepfather Allen at my bar mitzvah in 1967.

CHAPTER 9

Me and Juliet

Keep it gay, keep it light, keep it fresh, keep it fair
Let it bloom every night, give it room, give it air

—Oscar Hammerstein II and Richard Rodgers

The 1953 musical comedy *Me and Juliet* may not have been one of Rodgers and Hammerstein's best efforts as a team, but it has a pleasurable score. One song in particular, "Keep It Gay," became a hit whose lyric now can be misconstrued in a deliciously naughty fashion. Compare the lyric above with the song of the same title from Mel Brooks' *The Producers*:

> *No matter what you do on stage*
> *Keep it light, keep it bright, keep it gay!*

The lyrics of Mel Brooks are as innocent as Hammerstein's, yet the staging for the number was quite bawdy, with male chorus members performing some outrageous dry humping in rhythm. This, in turn, reminds me of George and Ira Gershwin's "I Got Rhythm."

> *I got rhythm, I got music,*
> *I got my man, who can ask for anything more.*

Indeed!

Sometimes it is not the content but the album cover that
stands out. This is one of my favorites: Ken Griffin playing
his organ for *The Happy Side*. The women appear to be
oblivious to the attraction their boyfriends have for each other.
My favorite selection is the almost autobiographical tune
"They'll Be Some Changes Made." Columbia CL 1518

As a child I spent too much time running away from being gay even
though it was quite inevitable. Choice? Hell no! Why would anyone choose to
be oppressed, ridiculed, and made to feel ashamed? Thankfully, great strides
have been made in my lifetime that I thought could never be possible. Gay
marriage? Unbelievable! Wonderful! Now we gay sinners can enjoy the same
benefits that the divorced and remarried sinners have long taken for granted.

I got married at the age of twenty-three to a lovely and talented girl whom
I met in a traveling company of *Godspell*. We actually sang in the same high
school chorus for a spell and were even partnered in an acting class a year or
so before we started dating. We were married for sixteen years in which we

produced one child, our son Drew. Twenty-odd years after our divorce, people still ask me why I married Donna. "I couldn't help myself," I reply honestly. She was just a fantastic person who could make me laugh and feel loved.

Although it appears that all of my relatives were perfectly aware of my gayness, my mother was in denial, perhaps even more than I was. Several years after meeting Dale, who at this writing has been my partner for over eighteen years, I decided to fly out to California to finally confront my mother with the truth. Dale warned me that it might not work in my favor, but I was tired of the deception and longed for a relationship with my parents that included Dale.

One particularly beautiful night I asked Mom if we could go for a walk alone. She looked at me inquisitively but remained silent, unusual for her, and walked with me as I bared my soul. "Why didn't you ever tell me?" she asked in the softest voice I ever heard come out of her mouth.

"I was afraid you would not love me anymore," I answered truthfully.

"Not love you?" she responded incredulously. "You're my Brucie. Nothing changes that." We walked around for another half hour as I allowed her to ask questions about my growing up and my marriage to Donna.

The next day I arrived at my parents' community pool late. As I entered the gate, I noticed Mom swimming on one of the flotation noodles and chatting with her girlfriends in the water. *Is she telling them what I told her last night? No, no, she wouldn't do that.* Then one of her friends gave me a knowing glance with a smile. *She told them! She told them in a few moments what it took me half a lifetime to admit!* I was so disappointed with her.

As my parents left me at the airport, my stepfather, Allen, gave me a hug and told me he loved me. He had never done that before unless pushed by Mom. Dale picked me up in Richmond, and on the way home I told him what had transpired and how upset I was that Mom had shared my news so quickly. "Oh Bruce, don't be upset with your mother," Dale said. "Don't you get it? Your mother is Jewish and you are gay. It's exotic. And now she no longer has to worry about another daughter-in-law."

I let it go, and a week later a letter arrived from Allen. Now, I had received letters from him before, but they were always in Mom's handwriting, and once in a while he would sign them. This letter was different. Allen wrote, "You are my son, and you will always be my son, and I don't care what you are."

Mom and Dale hit it off from the beginning. It was a relief not to hear her on the phone lamenting how unhappy she was because I was divorced and unmarried. "Now I just wish your brothers [divorced and straight] could be happy too."

"Mom, you know why I'm happy?" I kidded her.

"Why?" she asked, unprepared for my next line.

"Because I am gay. Ta-da!"

CHAPTER 10

The King and I

There are times I almost think
I am not sure of what I absolutely know

—Oscar Hammerstein II and Richard Rodgers

I WAS A LATE BLOOMER; my voice did not start to change until I was in the ninth grade. That was the year that my junior high school was producing *The King and I*. It was the year that no expense was spared on the lavish production. It was also the year that my voice cracked so much, I didn't even consider auditioning for the role of the king. Besides, one of my best friends, Patrick, was considered a shoo-in even before the auditions. He was funny, tall, very good looking, and a very good actor. No, I realized from the start that I was destined to play a very small role—the captain of the ship that brings Anna to Siam.

The musical director was Mrs. Weinberg, our music teacher, whom we all adored. Although possessed with a sweet disposition, she was firm and strong, and knew how to get the best out of our vocals. On the other hand, our director was a horror: an English teacher who was mean and scary and used intimidation to direct. We were all afraid of this woman. Expected to attend all rehearsals five days a week even if my character was not going to be used, I would hang out with my best friend, Steven, who was cast as one of the Siamese children.

On one particular Sunday morning, I noticed an ad in the Theater and Arts section of the *New York Times* that Sears was having a sale on the Rodgers and Hammerstein Deluxe Set, a three-record set that included the soundtracks from *The King and I, Oklahoma!* and *Carousel*. The problem was that the sale was only one day—Monday. This meant that I would have to leave right after school to get to Sears and then to the synagogue for my Hebrew lessons. In other words, I would need to skip a rehearsal. But how? Steven told me he would go with me to buy the records but didn't know how he was going to get out of rehearsal either. I decided I would make it the director's idea to tell me to leave the rehearsal.

The mono soundtrack LP of *The King and I* includes the full version of "Getting to Know You," but it was shortened on the stereo record. The same occurred with "The Carousel Waltz" in the mono LP of *Carousel*. Capitol W740

The next day, I took white chalk dust that had collected on the thin shelf below the blackboards and wiped it all over my face and neck so that I looked as pale as death. Then, just a few seconds before I walked into the rehearsal room, I rubbed my eyes violently until they appeared red and bloodshot. I opened the door slowly and moved lethargically to a front seat, apologizing for being late. "No problem," the director barked, and then continued with her spiel. Then suddenly she stopped barking and looked down on me. "Bruce, you look terrible. Are you all right?"

"I don't think so," I murmured in the tiniest voice in my repertoire.

"You need to go home right now. Steven, I'm not using you today. Would you mind going with Bruce since you live near him? I want him to get home safely."

I looked over at my best friend. "Well...okay," he answered without enthusiasm. Perfect—we had out-acted the acting teacher. Perhaps we had a future in theater.

We quietly left the room and walked down the hallway until we were around a corner. Then, fast as lightning, we ran out of the school, laughing and yelling all the way to the subway station. A half hour later we were in Sears and I bought my precious album. On the way home I opened the plastic wrap so we could read the insert and gaze at the photographs from the three films. When I arrived home, I discovered that the *Oklahoma!* vinyl was missing and in its place was a Christmas album by the Mormon Tabernacle Choir! I would have to make another trip to Sears to get a replacement.

The next day I did not show up to rehearsal at all, figuring that the director would think I was still sick. In fact, I spent the whole day in school making myself look ill, complaining about a fever. That way, no one could report, "Well, I saw Bruce today and he looked fine." When I got to Sears, the salesman asked me for my receipt, which I had in hand. But there were no more copies of the Rodgers and Hammerstein Deluxe Set, so he opened a soundtrack album of *Oklahoma!* and placed it in my album.

"There you go young man. How's that?"

"Thank you, sir," I said in the most innocent voice possible. How could I tell him how disappointed I was to have a record in the set with the wrong corresponding number on the vinyl? Or that I was disappointed with him as a record dealer for not knowing that substituting the wrong corresponding number record made that album less desirable?

I learned two lessons from this: neither my director nor the Sears salesman had my number, and skipping a rehearsal to buy a record is just wrong! Oh, and by the way, the student playing Sir Edward Ramsay was too ill to perform on opening night or during the run of the show. Guess who knew all of Ramsay's lines and substituted for him in addition to playing his own part?

CHAPTER 11

The Judy Garland Story

Shout hallelujah, c'mon get happy
You'd better chase all your cares away

—HAROLD ARLEN AND TED KOEHLER

EVEN BEFORE I ADMITTED TO myself that I was a "friend of Dorothy's" I knew that I was a friend of Judy's. Several times a month, with my other friends John and Phillip, I would raid the various record shops in Manhattan that specialized in soundtracks as well as original Broadway cast albums and, of course, Judy Garland records. John and Phillip would fight over the 78 rpm records by the Andrews Sisters while I was pretty much left alone to thumb through soundtracks and Garland records.

I miss record shops. Oh, yes, there are a few retro-type vinyl stores in nearby Richmond, Virginia, which is only about half an hour from where I live in Petersburg, but when I was a teenager growing up in New York City, there was an abundance of record shops. From the age of twelve in the mid-sixties until our last year in high school, my friends John and Phillip accompanied me—no, humored me—by allowing me to join them on record-hunting expeditions. One of our favorite haunts was Colony Records on Broadway to look but hardly ever buy, since they were too expensive for these junior high school boys and seemed to be geared as a tourist trap for the rich. Others included Bleecker Street Records, Second Hand Rose Music on Sixth Avenue, and Dayton Records in

A quintessential Judy Garland moment: performing "Get Happy" from her last MGM film, *Summer Stock* in 1950.

the Village, which had rare out-of-print soundtracks at decent prices. There was Downstairs Records in the train station at Forty-Second Street which favored 45 rpm records, and several other shops sprinkled throughout the city. Of course, there were also the Korvettes, Sears, Woolworths, and other department stores that featured record departments with "cut-out" records. Much later, when I was in my mid-twenties, Footlight Records, and Records Revisited, a record shop owned by Morton Savada and housed inside a skyscraper, were the only places left in Manhattan that specialized in 78 rpm records.

Each week John would look up record sales in the *Daily News* and I would do the same in the Sunday *New York Times* Arts section. Then we would trek to those record shops on the following Saturdays. My newspaper route afforded me a new record maybe once or twice a month (the rest of my salary had to go into the bank for college), but I always had a little left over for an egg cream or an Orange Julius with a fresh egg whipped in. Sometimes, John and Phillip would wear long trench coats so that a few Andrews Sisters 78s could be snugly stored when they lifted them while the record dealer wasn't looking. I must confess that I wanted to take records too. No, honesty had nothing to do with my staying on the right side of the law; it was just the fear of getting caught. Therefore, I was always something of an outsider, even though John was my best friend at the time. You see, John's best friend was Phillip and vice versa. There were, however, times when they became fierce rivals, fighting like cats when a rare Andrews Sisters record was within reach but only one of them could actually own it. It was then that John was closer to me, but it lasted only a few hours at most. Still, I spent many happy days with John either at my house or his, sharing our favorite records.

When the time came to decide what high schools we were going to attend, John and Phillip applied for and were accepted to the High School of Art and Design in Manhattan while I was delegated to New Dorp High School on Staten Island by my parents, who did not want their son commuting to school for a "commercial" degree. Ironically, I spent most of my high school weekends in Manhattan or at John's house in Brooklyn. Once a month or so, John would rearrange his parents' living room furniture and that of his bedroom. I remember coveting his stand-up, wind-up Victrola on which he would play Carmen Miranda; Maxine, Patty, and Laverne; and of course, Judy Garland. Most often we would hunker down in his bedroom listening to records, looking at movie books, and making recordings on his cassette player. The only self-recording I can remember with clarity was one that we made at my house with my reel-to-reel tape recorder. John played a record of Judy Garland singing "Over the Rainbow" in the background while we provided sound effects of a belligerent, drunken, Munchkin-sounding audience accented by clinking glasses and shouting obscenities to Judy's voice, as if she were performing "live" in a nightclub during her last years. The cruelty of youth, particularly for a future "friend" of Dorothy.

John and Phillip introduced me to Manhattan museums such as the Cloisters, the Metropolitan, and the Museum of Modern Art, as well as great old bookstores and head shops. No, we did not partake in the drugs, *honest*, but we loved the Peter Max posters, the incense, the Mae West and W. C. Fields posters, and the corner drugstores or Nedick's, where we would examine the records or books we had "acquired" and chat about them as we drank Coca-Cola, an orange drink, or an egg cream. Later those same evenings, I would go to bed with my new record or book lying near my pillow so that it would be the last thing I looked at before I went to sleep and the first thing I'd see in the morning. My favorite album was *The Judy Garland Story: The Star Years* on the MGM label, which I bought at Bleecker Street Records. The best song on that album was, and remains, my favorite recording of all time: "Get Happy." Strangely, when MGM Records released volume two, *The Hollywood Years*, they felt compelled to again add "Johnny One Note," one of Judy's least favorite songs, to the album.

By the time of Judy Garland's death in June 1969, my collection included *Judy Garland at Carnegie Hall, The Best of Judy Garland* on the Decca label, the Harmony Records rerelease of the soundtrack to *A Star Is Born,* and several 78 rpm record sets, including *Girl Crazy, Meet Me in St. Louis, The Harvey Girls,* and the *Judy Garland Second Souvenir Album*—all on the Decca label. I bought these last three albums in the Bronx from a former Decca employee who was selling his collection. John and Phillip bought out his Andrews Sisters 78s, all of which were pristine and even had the jagged edges that would ordinarily have been broken off before the records were cleaned and shipped out.

I bought *Girl Crazy* at the age of thirteen from Tassie's, a gas station just two blocks from where I lived on Staten Island. John had written to a columnist of *The New York Daily News* expressing his interest in the Andrews Sisters, asking anyone with old 78s to please give him a call. John's phone number was actually in the article! Within a few days, he had received several calls from readers all around the city, including the Decca employee mentioned above and the owner of Tassie's Service Station. The owner, a sixtyish auto mechanic who was unshaved and unkempt, led us through his service garage to a small, filthy storage room in the back where several hundred records lay in dust. Although John immediately found several Andrews Sisters records, I looked in vain for any by Garland.

"How much?" John asked as he piled up a dozen or so shellacs.

On November 26, 1943, MGM released *Girl Crazy* which
was to become the last in the series of the Judy/Mickey
musicals. A few weeks earlier Judy Garland, Mickey Rooney,
and a twenty-eight-piece orchestra led by the film's conductor
Georgie Stoll recorded the songs from the film for Decca
Records. Among the great Gershwin tunes, the album features
a sublime version of "Embraceable You" by Judy and a witty
duet by the co-stars in "Could You Use Me?" Decca 362

"Fifty cents each," Mr. Tassie replied. After thirty minutes of searching I was still empty-handed. John was about to pay for his treasures when Mr. Tassie asked what I collected.

"Judy Garland!" I professed proudly.

"Well, I might just have something that you want right here on this desk," Mr. Tassie assured me as he wiped away layers of grimy dust and ledgers. I must confess that I was skeptical of wanting anything he found in his dirt pile, but he pulled out an almost mint copy of *Girl Crazy* with Mickey Rooney and Judy Garland, adding, "But this set will cost you a little more than your friend is paying for his Andrews Sisters records." I gulped as I held the beautiful album with its wonderful cover photo of Rooney and Garland riding a rocking horse. I was too afraid to ask. "Six dollars; this one is six dollars. That's two dollars for each record and I'll throw in the album cover for free. It's my favorite."

I reached into my pocket. That is exactly what I had. We had been planning to use some of that money to buy Dunkin' Donuts and chocolate milk just a few blocks up on Hylan Boulevard, but I quickly gave old man Tassie the money before he changed his mind. *Girl Crazy* became one of my favorite record sets. I can't recall who wrote that "George and Ira Gershwin never had it so good," but I remember playing those 78s at least twice a week for several months. For many years I sought out the ten-inch LP and the 45 rpm EP versions of that album, but when I finally purchased them on eBay, I was utterly disappointed by the album covers, which were rather generic compared with the graphics and images of young Judy and Mickey from the film on the original Decca release.

By the time I was in my late teens, I was obsessed with owning all of Judy's records in their various formats, even collecting cassettes and eight-track tapes until I quickly deemed them inferior to vinyl. It was as if I alone were preserving her records for posterity.

Fanatic, you say? No, just a friend. And an addict.

CHAPTER 12

Good News

The moon belongs to everyone
The best things in life are free

—LYRICS BY B. G. DESYLVA AND LEW BROWN,
MUSIC BY RAY HENDERSON

MY SECOND LOVE WAS JUNE Allyson.

"Who was June Allyson?" you ask. Why, she was just about the cutest thing in movies walking on two feet, a genuine June bug and cute as a bug's ear! From the early 1940s through the mid-fifties, June Allyson was America's sweetheart, MGM's girl next door, the perfect ingénue, and later, the perfect screen wife. Of course I was aware of the discrepancies in our ages; I was barely twelve years old, whereas June was thirty-six years older. Still, I was tall for my age, easily reaching her five-foot-one height. There was hope.

My introduction to June on vinyl occurred when I bought the used soundtrack album to *Till the Clouds Roll By* while in the eighth grade. The album was part of a series of soundtracks that MGM reissued in 1960 as "Original Cast" albums. The reality, though, was that many of the recordings were not original cast albums, not as soundtracks or as Broadway cast albums. *Good News, Rose Marie, The Merry Widow,* and *Showboat* were all remakes.

I did not know about the LP that paired *Good News* with *Words and Music* until I was a tenth grader living on Staten Island. As a graduation present from

51

junior high school I was given five dollars so I could buy the *Words and Music* soundtrack album on four 78s. That summer my parents forbade me to go into the city because of some extremely violent race riots. In the fall I bought the 78s to *Good News* starring June Allyson, Peter Lawford, Joan McCracken, and Ray McDonald. During the run of *A Party with Betty Comden and Adolph Green*, the lyricists/screenplay writers quipped about their adaptation of the classic college musical. "Good News was never a picture we were entirely happy with," confided Comden to the "live" audience on the album. "We used to say there were the big three of cinematic history: *Potemkin*, *Intolerance*, and *Good News*." Although *Good News* does not top many lists in any category of films, it is nonetheless a fun and well-constructed musical comedy that works in all departments thanks to Charles Walters' quick paced direction.

The original soundtrack of *Good News* was first released as a four 78 rpm record album in 1947. It was later released on a ten-inch LP and as a four 45 rpm record set in 1950 as seen in the illustration here. MGM K17

I must have listened to that record set a hundred times until I came across a record shop on the Island that specialized in hard-to-find LPs. You can't imagine how elated I was when I asked the shopkeeper if it was possible to order a copy of *Good News* coupled with *Words and Music* on a long-playing record and he replied that he could pick one up in the city for me for six dollars. *Where the hell was he going to buy it?* "The warehouse," he replied. Was there really a warehouse in Manhattan that sold out-of-print records? The next week he presented me with a sealed copy! I paid the six dollars for the album and purchased a sealed mono copy of the soundtrack of *Bells Are Ringing* for an additional four dollars. Though I had to leave my Brooklyn paper route when my family moved, a Staten Island route easily supported what was becoming the addictive habit of collecting show tunes.

What was it that made *Good News* one of my favorite MGM musicals even before I saw it many years later? Yes, I really liked June Allyson, but even in my worst fan mode I recognized that she wasn't the best singer in the world. Nor, for that matter, was Peter Lawford, yet somehow his songs were charming and quite listenable, especially "Be a Ladies' Man" with new lyrics by Comden and Green which they adapted from "He's a Ladies Man." At the time I had no idea that it was the considerable contributions of Mel Tormé in the chorus, Kay Thompson's fine harmonizing vocal arrangements, and the conducting of the MGM orchestra by Lennie Hayton. How could I know? First of all, despite Mel Tormé's vocal presence in "Be a Ladies' Man," he is given no recording credit on the album, nor is Ray McDonald, whose voice is also recognizable. Nor do the other singers receive any billing—including the Williams Brothers, as in Andy Williams. And nowhere on any soundtrack record of the period is Kay Thompson's name to be found. No, Thompson, like many vocal arrangers of the period, received a healthy weekly check from MGM but no credit. Because I had recognized orchestra conductor Lennie Hayton's name from other soundtrack albums such as *Singin' in the Rain* and *Words and Music*, I simply assumed that it was he who created the MGM sound I so craved. It was not until later that the names Conrad Salinger and Johnny Green meant anything.

There was also another voice on the soundtrack, not quite as polished as Allyson's but far and away better than Lawford's. Joan McCracken! I had heard of her before. She was the girl who purposely fell down during a number from the Broadway show *Oklahoma!* Her two vocals on that *Good News* soundtrack—she's heard briefly in the title song but has much more time in "Pass That Peace Pipe"—are so full of unbridled energy and enthusiasm that her untrained voice becomes a prime asset to her interpretation of the songs. Several years were to pass before I was able to actually see the film and witness her terpsichorean talents; she was one of the few true musical comedy performers in *Good News*. The other was Ray McDonald. Yes, Patricia Marshall was in the film too, but her singing, although better than that of most of her costars, excluding Tormé, was lacking in any memorable characteristics, making her solos merely functionary.

But June was my favorite back in the day. My confession? Junie appeared on a 1968 episode of the popular NBC series *Name of the Game*, playing the mother of a drug addict. That evening I took photographs of the actress in a blond wig with my cheap camera. I gave the roll of film and four dollars to my stepfather, whose cousins owned a camera shop that also developed film. What I did not know was that they processed the film in their shop rather than sending it out. A week later my stepfather reprimanded me for wasting film and money. I asked him how I had done that, and he replied that his cousins told him I had taken pictures of Doris Day from a television set. I was furious. Not only were the pictures paid for from my newspaper route, but more importantly, the images were of June Allyson. Not Doris Day. The morons!

CHAPTER 13

Best Foot Forward

I love the boogie 'cause it tickles my spine
I love the boogie 'cause it's fresh and it's fine

—HUGH MARTIN AND RALPH BLAINE

I WAS FAMILIAR WITH THE songs of most of the musical films of the forties and fifties long before I ever saw the films themselves. *Best Foot Forward* is a perfect example. My stepdad's cousins lived a few doors down the street from us on Staten Island. Because I was the only responsible high school teenager in the neighborhood, I had a very lucrative business babysitting for them as well as for three or four other households. This was especially fun on weekdays because I could do my homework while watching television, which was not allowed at home, and have all the soda, ice cream, and various chips and cookies I could eat. My neighbors were always generous in that respect, and I earned $1.75 an hour! Yet the most lingering gift was not intentional.

One day while I was babysitting, Don, my stepfather's cousin through marriage, placed a neat, two-foot pile of 78 rpm records on the street for pickup by the department of sanitation. Not knowing what they were, but sensing that they were something special, I schlepped the records home and began playing them on our turntable. The singers and songs were incredible: there was Doris Day, Frank Sinatra, Bing Crosby, the Andrews Sisters, Betty Hutton, a record from *Oklahoma!* featuring Celeste Holme singing "All or

Nothin'" and two Nancy Walker recordings on the RCA label, "Just a Little Joint with a Juke Box" and "Shady Lady Bird," from a show called *Best Foot Forward*. It would be a few years before I would obtain her other record of songs from the musical as well as the Martins' songs on Capitol Records and Tommy Dix singing "Buckle Down Winsocki" with the Benny Goodman Orchestra.

One night, a few weeks after finding my treasure, I was vigorously studying my weekly TV guide to see what musicals I might tape on my cassette recorder when I noticed that the 1943 film adaptation of *Best Foot Forward* was playing on television, at 2:00 a.m., on a school night! Thus Operation Late, Late Show began what would be the first of many nights I would pretend to go to sleep and then sneak downstairs to the family room in the basement to record a film. Placing the microphone next to the television speaker, I recorded the entire film soundtracks, dialogue and all, on my cassette recorder. A few years later my parents purchased a portable black-and-white TV with an earphone outlet, making it easier to record directly with a much cleaner sound.

The primary attraction of *Best Foot Forward* was that the film starred, among others, June Allyson in her first movie role. Snatched up from the Broadway cast by MGM producer Arthur Freed (along with Nancy Walker, Tommy Dix, Kenny Bowers, and Jack Jordan), June sang one of the highlights of the film, "The Three B's," which she shared with Nancy Walker and newcomer Gloria DeHaven. The song is a delightful medley of three songs, "The Barrelhouse, the Boogie Woogie, and the Blues." Walker warbles a deadpan delivery of the boogie portion of the song, Gloria's glides through the blues section, and June's knocks the barrelhouse à la Betty Hutton, whom she had understudied on Broadway. Audiences would witness that same frenetic style later that year in *Girl Crazy*, when she tossed Mickey Rooney around a nightclub set while warbling "Treat Me Rough."

June and Gloria were also featured in the opening number "Wish I May," which, incidentally, featured a very young Stanley Donen before he became one of Hollywood's best directors. But it was Nancy Walker who stole the film from veterans Lucille Ball, William Gaxton, and Virginia Weidler with

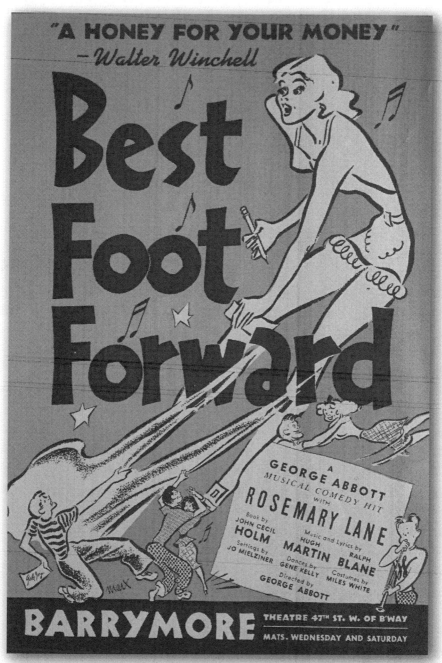

A 1941 flyer advertising the Broadway musical *Best Foot Forward*.

her duet "Alive and Kickin'" with none other than Harry James. James, who was extremely popular with bobbysoxers, played the perfect straight man to Walker's hilarious and joyous antics as she sang and danced rings around him. Because Walker was only four foot eight or so compared with the tall and lanky James, the sight of these two performers side by side is in itself hysterical, but the tiny performer made the most of the number with an ease that belied her age. Unfortunately, except for appearances in *Girl Crazy*, *Broadway Rhythm* with her show stopping "Milkman, Keep Those Bottles Quiet!" and a really bad Doris Day film, *Lucky Me*, Hollywood never took advantage of her versatility. Thank goodness for Broadway and, much later, television.

In 1993, "The Three B's" was not only one of the high points of *That's Entertainment Part III*, but also received its first legitimate release on a commercial soundtrack album. It took another decade for Rhino Records to release the full soundtrack of *Best Foot Forward* complete with musical cues and outtakes. The CD features an overture in addition to the instrumental music of the opening credits. Even more interesting are the "techie" liner notes in which Rhino says the overture was recorded on July 1, 1943, even though the film opened at the Astor Theatre in New York City the day before.

Also included is a cute duet of "What Do You Think I Am?" with June Allyson and Kenny Bowers. The liner notes say that the song was written especially for the film and then cut, but sheet music from the 1941 Broadway production suggests otherwise, not to mention the *Playbill*. In 1963 Liza Minnelli performed the song in an Off-Broadway revival.

How does the film stand up after all these years? The comedy portions with Lucille Ball are still humorous, and each member of the youthful cast contributes much of the charm, fun, and infectious qualities of the film. The CD, now out of print, also boasts the talents of Jeanne Durrell, dubbing for Virginia Wielder singing "Ev'ry Time," Gloria Grafton ghosting for Lucille Ball on "You're Lucky," Helen Forrest and B. Saul singing "Shady Lady Bird," Harry James's famous "Flight of the Bumblebee," and Tommy Dix in the megahit "Buckle Down Winsocki." Incidentally, "The Main Title," "The Three B's," "Alive and Kickin'," and an alternative take of "Wish I May" are in stereo. According to Rhino Records, only 2,500 CDs were issued online, each with a number representing its limited edition. So if you can find it, buy it! Mine is number 241. After my purchase the cassette version I recorded so long ago was given to the sanitation department just as my father's cousin had tried to do with his 78s. Déjà vu!

Kenny Bowers and June Allyson performing "What Do You Think I Am?" from the 1941 Broadway production of *Best Foot Forward*.

CHAPTER 14

Those Glorious
MGM Musicals

I guess I'll have to change my plan
I never knew that there could be another man

—FROM *THE BAND WAGON* BY HOWARD DIETZ AND ARTHUR SCHWARTZ

YOU HAVE ALREADY READ THAT I used to sleep with my records. I would gaze lovingly at the covers, read the liner notes, and feel the glossy finish on the jackets. I was eleven years old, and right from the beginning I was a hard-core MGM junkie. The MGM soundtracks were my favorites. Not just the reissues, mind you. No, I had to have the originals! The earliest LP album covers were quite attractive with their photographs and catchy graphics, but they had this thin glossy coat of plastic that made each album cover shimmer like a jewel. If the record jacket was in poor shape, the plastic could be peeled off, revealing a pristine image underneath.

The problem with collecting MGM soundtracks was that there were numerous releases on all the various formats since they were first introduced in 1947 with *Till the Clouds Roll By*. There were 78 rpm record sets, the ten-inch albums, the 45 rpm record sets, the "extended-play" 45s, the abbreviated double-soundtrack LPs from 1956, and finally, the complete double soundtracks in 1960. These last are among my favorites, because each record contains two complete soundtracks that were released as "original cast albums," no doubt an attempt by the record company to make them seem more like a prestigious original Broadway cast recording. In the seventies, with the unexpected success of the MGM compilation film *That's Entertainment,* many of the albums were again reissued in the United States and in Britain. There were also eight-track-tape versions, but they were for amateurs, because they often changed the sequence of the songs and would even interrupt a song to change tracks. Okay, I'll admit it: I did buy a few of the eight-tracks years later as souvenirs, but I got rid of them when my partner, Dale, pressed the issue: "It's either eight-tracks or me! You must maintain standards in your collecting."

MGM's Silver Anniversary was celebrated in 1949
with this rare 78 rpm record set that has never
been released on any other format. MGM 42

When *That's Entertainment* was playing at the Ziegfeld Theatre in New York, I couldn't wait to see it. I went with my friend Fred; with whom I was desperately in love. We were both actors in a musical, *100 Hundred Miles from Nowhere* (which is exactly where it went), at the now famous 13th Street Repertory Theatre. The theater was owned and managed by Edith O'Hara and upon opening in 1972 became a haven for young actors arriving in New York City. It is now famous as the home of the longest-running Off-Off-Broadway play, Israel Horvitz's *Line*, but in the early seventies it was known for presenting musicals by new and unknown writers and composers. *One Hundred Miles from Nowhere* was written by Donald Ward and the theater's resident artist, Bill Solly, a songwriter who is particularly adept at writing clever lyrics and memorable melodies. Edith lived in a flat upstairs, and there was also a dorm-like space for the young actors in her productions. Each show was allocated fifty dollars for scenery and costumes, with the cast members supplying most of their costumes.

A sophomore in college, I auditioned during a September casting call, singing "Magic Changes" from *Grease*. Earlier that week I had also tried out for replacements for *The Fantasticks* on Sullivan Street as well as *Grease* on Broadway. Edith sat in the small theater with one of her best actors, Raymond Wood, who would soon become a close friend and confidante. The musical had already been playing two years at the theater, so I was cast as a general understudy but appeared nightly for a few minutes in a dance sequence for a number called "July the First." My call was at 7:00 p.m., but I was allowed to leave after the first act, although I often stayed later to hang out with fellow cast members on the roof of the theater.

The musical was revamped in the summer of 1974 and recast with me being the only holdover. Twenty years old and, as Raymond referred to me, a neuter, I found myself attracted to new cast member Fred, who was twenty going on thirty. He was an extremely talented actor who could sing and dance. He was also cute as a button—a Jewish button. A few inches shorter than me, he had a thin but strong-looking body, and a head of curly black hair. Although Fred was less than a year older than me, he was much wiser and more sophisticated. He was also the first boy I ever kissed.

Having grown up hiding my attraction to my own sex, it was quite a relief to open up with Raymond when I stayed at the theater one night to work on masks for a children's show. "I've noticed that the two of you hang out, and I approve," he said to me. "He's a darling young man. But I really didn't think you were attracted to men...or women for that matter. Are you sure?"

"I'm pretty sure," I answered nervously. "When did you first know?"

"I always knew. There was never any doubt. As for you, be careful. Fred looks experienced."

"He's also very handsome!" I added quickly.

"Now, now," Raymond assured me. "You're handsome too, especially with your new short haircut. You look quite hunky, and he looks quite divine. You know what to do?"

I didn't. I didn't know how to tell Fred I liked him. I also didn't know what two men did "behind closed doors" and really didn't care until I met Fred. Then I knew I needed to find out, and damn quick too. One Thursday night during a rehearsal, the director informed us that we would be rehearsing late on Friday night as well as have an early call on Saturday morning. I was commuting to Staten Island from my Manhattan college on weekends, and really not looking forward to several subway and ferry rides in such a short time period. Knowing that Fred lived in Manhattan and how nice he had been to me, I was able to get him to ask me to stay overnight. *Yes!*

That Friday night, rehearsal seemed to last forever. All I could think of was being with Fred. Much to my chagrin, when we finally arrived at Fred's apartment in Hell's Kitchen, he prepared the couch in his living room with sheets and a pillow and then, kissing me on the forehead like a father, retired to his bedroom. *How am I going to get Fred to invite me in there?* I had to think fast before he fell asleep. Waiting no more than five minutes, I called out, "Are you asleep?"

"Not yet," he responded. "I need to unwind a bit."

"Me too," I added. "I'm having trouble sleeping out here. It's so strange to sleep in a place you've never slept before."

The next few seconds seemed like an eternity, but finally Fred asked the question I had been waiting for: "Do you want to sleep in here with me?" *Eureka!*

"You wouldn't mind?" I asked as sheepishly as possible.

"No, come on in." As I climbed into his bed, he pulled the covers over us, placed his arms around me, and gave me an affectionate squeeze. We spoke softly with a lovely intimacy I had never experienced before. At some point, finally, we kissed. There have been other loves in my life before and since, but that first kiss with a sweet boy named Fred was the most dangerous kiss I ever experienced. *Oh my God, this is what it's supposed to be like!*

The next few weeks were an incredible journey as I spent every possible moment with Fred. I invited him to my parents' house on Staten Island to stay overnight so we could go to the beach, we saw the second acts of several Broadway shows by walking in with the crowds during intermission, and I introduced Fred to Coney Island. My only disappointment with him was his less-than-enthusiastic response to the film *That's Entertainment*, which was playing at the Ziegfeld Theatre.

"Too much dancing," he said flatly at the end of the picture. *Too much dancing?* As far as I was concerned, there was not enough. For my young readers, you have to remember that this was decades before home videos and that the only way to get a fix of vintage musical films was through art houses in major cities. I still regret that I was not able to see *Kiss Me Kate* in 3-D in a New York 3-D film festival, although I own a rare original poster advertising it in 3-D and it was recently released on Blu-ray in 3-D as well as the flat version.

I could not wait to buy the soundtrack from *That's Entertainment*, but to my horror, it was released on MCA Records! *MCA? What happened to the MGM label? Why weren't all those MGM songs being issued on their own label?* Fortunately, shortly after I bought the two-record set I found a Canadian pressing on the MGM label, produced by Polydor records. It even included an insert that the MCA release lacked.

If you have noticed the abrupt shift in subject matter, it is because as I was falling head over heels in love with Fred, he told me that he had a boyfriend on, of all places, Staten Island! He was a musician who played the organ for a Catholic church. I met him and even stayed at the rectory one night, sleeping on the floor while Fred and his organ player slept on the bed next to me. It was pure torture.

The show *100 Hundred Miles from Nowhere* closed unexpectedly after losing several performers moments before the curtain went up. Fred and I remained friends, but he went on to other plays while I became more involved in college productions, pottery, and sculpture. But I'll never forget that day at the beach when he told me that I would always remember him. He was right. When I fell in love with Donna, and wanted to marry her, Fred warned me to be cautious, as did Raymond. But I would hear none of it. "Love transcends sexuality!" I roared. Raymond nodded knowingly, because he had been in a marriage that hadn't worked out. As for Fred, he met his life partner shortly afterward and they are still together. We chat on the phone occasionally and exchange Christmas cards and e-mails once in a while. I even stayed with them in their beautiful home for a week a few years ago.

Donna and I had been married for sixteen years when she called it quits. Our son, Drew, ten at the time, took it well. Donna accepted a great-paying position in Virginia, and although I had never had any desire to live in the South, I guess I changed my plans, because I was positive that there would never be another woman...or man. Donna wed two years later, and another year after that, I met Dale.

CHAPTER 15

Mame

We need a little Christmas
Right this very minute

—Jerry Herman

From the age of seventeen, I had always been quite fortunate in that I could work anywhere, which was good since I could never face my parents and family without the prospects of a job. Actually, Mom secured a job for each of her sons once we turned sixteen. While I was attending Hunter College in the 1970s, I applied to the Doubleday Book Shops on Fifth Avenue because I could not think of a better job for a college student than working in a sophisticated bookshop. Also, and equally important, Doubleday stocked all these great MGM soundtrack imports from England, which, with my employee's discount, would have been a terrific bonus. And, oh yes, the stores were eleven blocks from my school. Perfect!

Unfortunately, there was a waiting list, and it was not until I was teaching five years later that I was finally called to come in for an interview. However, upon graduation from graduate school (with honors!), I could not find a job in my field (pottery and sculpture), so I went to the LaMar Employment Agency in Manhattan, which immediately placed me in a music library. I was thrilled. It was one of those theater rental libraries that control the rights to produce musicals, amateur and professional. Later I found out that the

French-sounding agency was really made up by combining the first names of the two owners—Larry and Margaret.

The original Broadway cast album of *Mame* features a great
Jerry Herman score, Angela Lansbury, Beatrice Arthur,
and Jane Connell. The film soundtrack with Lucille Ball
has only three things going for it: Jerry Herman's score,
Beatrice Arthur, and Jane Connell. Columbia KOS 3000

I stuck with my job at the music library for nine months. The pay was excellent, the hours were regular, and there was even a Christmas bonus. Our job, one of the most boring in the industry, was to pick up rental contracts from a box in the mailroom and then pull the conductors' scores, separate instrumental parts, scripts, directors' manuals, and cue booklets from the vast shelves in the building and bring them to the packers. If the scores or scripts were heavily marked in pencil, we would have to erase them first. And, on a bad day, when hardly any scores were going out, we would have to spend hours just erasing and erasing. On any given day you could find an employee on a fifteen-minute break in the restroom just to escape the monotony. Once in a great while one of us might be asked to retrieve a rare script or piece of music from the basement. This was a treat, because as you were searching for the material requested, you were skimming through the history of the American musical theater.

To assure that management got all they could from their employees, they worked out a deal that if we came to work half an hour earlier, we would receive a pastry, doughnut, bagel, or roll, and a juice or coffee. But then there would be no breaks during the day except for lunch.

Somehow, despite it being the world's most boring job and despite the knowledge that I was "going nowhere fast"—to take a line from James Mason about his career before *A Star Is Born*—there were laughs and fun. I met a couple of opera singers, Rob and Dianna, a husband and wife who supported their musical studies with this non-challenging daytime job. And then there was Raymond, our mailroom manager.

Raymond was *something else*, even in the late seventies, when *something else* was constantly being redefined. A tall, pale, white man with thinning brown hair and a thick mustache, Raymond was a conglomerate of all the Village People singers except, perhaps, for the American Indian, but he was more dignified. He would walk with quick, small strides, his hands anxiously fluttering about in stereo while his deep theatrical voice boomed management's commands. Totally lacking in humor, Raymond's life seemed to be an open book, at least for those working under him. He was also generous to a fault, giving his workers tickets to plays, concerts, and recitals. The first time he offered me free tickets was to a concert with André Previn conducting the Boston Symphony at Carnegie Hall. I looked at him with suspicion, but he said drily, "Don't worry; I don't want to sleep with you. I just thought you would appreciate the tickets." And I did! I had never been to Carnegie Hall. It was a thrill. Of course, I was even more elated because this was the same André Previn who had conducted the orchestras for such films as *Gigi* and *My Fair Lady*, and composed the scores to *It's Always Fair Weather* and *Inside Daisy Clover*. I appreciated Raymond's generosity and came to realize that under his flamboyant and often bitchy exterior was a queen with a heart of gold. Therefore, despite the many times I was egged on by my friends to inquire about Raymond's coat, I decided that I was not going to contribute to the laughs. Fortunately, I did not have to wait long.

"Would you like to see my Christmas tree?" Raymond asked one day in mid-December.

"I'd love to, Raymond, but I always meet my father-in-law downtown after work on Fridays. Could we make it another time?"

"Oh no, silly, I wasn't inviting you to my home. I just wanted to know if you would like to see my tree."

"Okay…" I answered. "Do you have photos or something?"

"Exactly!" he replied, glowing more brightly than any Christmas tree lights could possibly compete with. "Here they are!" With that Raymond pulled four or five small snapshots out of his wallet. The tree was indeed beautiful, well designed with its lights, ornaments, beads and…but what was that? My eyes were diverted to each side of the tree where a group of large chains and long leather belts hung in support of the symmetrical composition of the photo. "Oh those," he said nonchalantly as if reading my mind. "Those are my whips and chains." Trying my best not to act shocked or be judgmental, I quickly took note of a coat hanging nearby and murmured, "Nice coat!"

"Oh, my coat, yes. Has anyone told you anything about my coat?"

"Not that I can remember," I lied. "I don't think it has ever come up in conversation."

"Well, let me be the first to tell you, then. It was about two years ago around Christmastime, and I brought this guy home for the night. He was very cute with long blond hair and a great body, and we had a wonderful evening. But when I woke up the next morning, I discovered that he was dead."

"Dead?" I asked quietly.

"Yes, dead as a doornail!"

"Yikes!" I exclaimed, still not sure where this was going. "And he was dead…in your bed? Sorry, I didn't mean to make that rhyme."

"Exactly! And I might use that rhyme the next time I'm telling this story. Anyway, I dressed him, as I thought that was the proper thing to do…"

Raymond paused until I nodded in agreement. "And then I called the police to have his body removed. However, I really liked his coat and thought that where he was going, he wouldn't really need it anymore. I mean, it fit me perfectly well, so it would have been a waste of a perfectly good coat." Raymond looked me directly in the eyes. "Do you think it was wrong?"

"No, of course not," I replied. Actually, what I was wondering at that moment was just when Raymond had tried on this dead man's coat. *Oh my, my trick is dead! I think I'll try on his coat!* or *I'll try on his coat right after I dress him* or *I'll try it on just before I call the police.* "But didn't the police want to know if he was wearing a coat when he arrived at your apartment? I mean, wasn't it cold outside?"

"Hmm," he said, and thought for a few seconds. "No one has ever asked that before." Then, after another thoughtful moment he gushed, "Now, wasn't that a nice Christmas present?"

CHAPTER 16

It's Better with a Band

Sing a song with me to ease your worries…
Sing a song with me to move the heavens.

—Wally Harper and Paul Zakrzewski

I discovered Barbara Cook around 1982. Now, when I say I discovered Barbara Cook, what I mean is that I heard one of her albums, not that I actually discovered her. Miss Cook had already been around Broadway since 1950, although in the late seventies she made a smooth and triumphant transition to cabaret and concert halls, beloved by New Yorkers and Londoners for a voice and delivery that could probably move the heavens.

I had seen a few of her Columbia albums in the record stores and knew that she was in the Broadway musical *The Music Man,* in 1959, but I had never really thought of her as a singer whose albums one might buy. However, an album titled *Barbara Cook—It's Better with a Band* was recorded "live" at Carnegie Hall in the then-new digital sound. *What was this digital sound?* Without listening to any of her other records, I bought the album for $9.99, a hefty sum for a record then, and brought it home only to be blown away by the clarity and strength of the opening orchestra number. Then, and quite unexpectedly, I was further entranced by Miss Cook's delivery of "I Love a Piano," by Irving Berlin. At once she was the loveliest soprano I had ever heard: pure, with extraordinary phrasing and intonation; sophisticated yet friendly; swinging, sassy, and sexy too. In short, Barbara Cook was and remains my favorite soprano. I even met her. Twice!

It's Better with a Band is a recorded concert given by Barbara Cook at Carnegie Hall in 1981. The album is an early digital recording on vinyl. Moss Music Group MMG-104

The first time was in 1990 when she appeared as a guest artist in Mel Tormé's *Twelve Nights of Christmas* series in New Jersey. During the intermission, I went backstage and introduced myself, totally ignoring the fact that she was in pain from a chronic back problem. Never mind that she needed to rest for the upcoming second act; it was all about me. A decade later I caught her act at Lincoln Center, and this time, older and wiser, I waited outside the stage door to say hello. She walked out and was quickly surrounded by a dozen or so fans, each asking for her autograph, yet somehow, I was able to reach her before she departed in the waiting limousine.

"I just wanted to tell you how wonderful you are and how you have en-riched my life with your singing," I said calmly, trying to hide the excitement I was feeling.

"Well, thank you very much," she replied graciously.

"And I want to apologize for being such an inconsiderate fan years ago when you sang with Mel Tormé."

"How's that?" She surprised me.

"I came backstage to introduce myself, knowing full well that you were suffering from back pain, not allowing you to take the break you needed dur-ing intermission."

"Oh my," she answered quickly. "Thank you. Would you like me to sign your program?"

Suddenly—and I don't know where my answer came from—I simply said, "Oh no, I don't need your autograph. I heard you sing tonight and that is plenty enough." She smiled, grasping my hand, expressed her thanks, and then climbed into her limo, which drove away into the anonymity that is New York City.

Actually, I was supposed to see Barbara Cook sing at the famed Rainbow Room a year earlier as a thirty-ninth birthday present from Donna, my wife at the time. A couple of weeks before the event Donna told me that she had made reservations for that Friday evening, an unusually cold night for November 13. Arriving late from the school where I taught in New Jersey, I walked into the house upset that I still had not found the time to buy the proper tie to wear with my suit that night. You had to wear a tie in the Rainbow Room. Donna told me not to worry, that in fact she had purchased a tie for me earlier that day and that all I needed to do was take a hot bath and relax.

"But we'll be late!" I exclaimed.

"Not to worry—everything will be fine," she assured me calmly. A few minutes later, as I was soaking in the most wonderful bath, Donna rushed into the bathroom. "Your brother's car has broken down in Stapleton and he needs help!" Stapleton is about twenty minutes from New Dorp, where we lived in Staten Island.

"Stapleton!" I practically shouted. "That's on the other side of the island! We'll miss Barbara Cook!"

Again, Donna was most reassuring. "I'll iron your shirt and have your new tie and suit ready for you as soon as you get back. Don't worry; we won't be late."

Grabbing whatever I could to cover myself from the cold, I drove to Stapleton, where I found Mark's car parked in front of a bar. I must tell you that Stapleton was not exactly the safest place to be at night, certainly not in a bar. There was no sign of Mark, so I stepped into the bar only to find him playing pool at the other end. "Wanna play a game?" he asked me in a most casual manner.

"No," I replied irritably. "We're going to see Barbara Cook tonight! What's wrong anyway?"

"My car needs a jump. Do you have cables?"

"Yes, and lucky for you! Why didn't you tell Donna what was wrong? I might not have had the cables with me tonight."

"I knew you would have them. You want a drink?"

"No, I don't want a drink! You know I don't drink! Besides, we're going to see Barbara Cook tonight!"

"Okay, okay. C'mon," he replied as he led me back outside. I drove my car to meet his and then gave him the jump for his battery.

"There! Now, don't stop anywhere until you get home," I instructed him.

"I think you should follow me, just in case I break down again."

"Follow you? We're going to see Barbara Cook tonight! I can't follow you!"

"Please follow me, Bruce. I'm worried that it could happen again."

"This is crazy," I retorted. "What were you doing in Stapleton?"

"A business meeting," he replied flatly.

"All right, okay. Let's get going, though. I don't want to be late for Barbara Cook! Donna must have spent a fortune for our tickets."

I followed my brother's car, getting even more frustrated at how slowly he was driving. Finally arriving at his house, he stepped out of his car and approached my window, signaling me to roll it down. "You wanna come in and warm up?"

"NO! WE'RE GOING TO SEE BARBARA COOK TONIGHT!"

"Okay, okay, calm your cookies. I'll call Donna and tell her you're on your way. Don't drive too fast."

Don't drive too fast? I thought to myself. *We're never going make it. We're going miss Barbara Cook!* I looked at Mark as I was closing the window and calmed down. "Don't go anywhere until you get a new battery, Mark. Night." Mark and Sharon lived about twenty minutes from our house. Perhaps, with any luck, we could still make it to see some of Barbara Cook's performance.

Arriving home in record time—I am usually a very slow driver—I jumped out of my car and ran as fast as I could to the front door, out of breath and shivering. The door was locked, so I rang the doorbell, thinking to myself, *We* are *going to see Barbara Cook tonight! We* are *going to make it!*

Donna answered the door, and as I stepped inside the house, noting for the first time that it was unusually dark, the lights suddenly turned on as friends and relatives shouted at the top of their lungs, "SURPRISE!" I looked at them, then at Donna, whom I proceeded to drag outside while I closed the front door. "Does that mean we're not seeing Barbara Cook tonight?"

CHAPTER 17

Alice in Wonderland

How d'ye do and shake hands
State your name and business.

—Oliver Wallace and Cy Coben

"Do you like tea?"

"Oh yes!" I replied into my telephone. "I love tea!"

"Well, then, you will have to come over so we can chat awhile and have some tea and biscuits. But I must warn you that I tire easily, so I am not sure how much time we can spend together. Is that all right with you?"

"Oh yes—whatever works for you."

And that is how I met "the other Wendy." For almost a year I had tried to interview Eva Le Gallienne, one of the greatest actresses of the American theater, for a book I was writing on *Peter Pan*. Le Gallienne, or, as her friends called her, LeG, was considered the equal of Helen Hayes and Katherine Cornell during the 1920s when she conquered Broadway with her performances in *Liliom* and *The Swan*. Although she could choose whatever role she wanted to play on Broadway, LeG gave it up to establish the Civic Repertory Theatre, a company of accomplished actors such as Walter Beck, Leona Roberts, Joseph Schildkraut, and Richard Waring as well as up-and-coming youngsters such as Burgess Meredith, Howard da Silva, and future writer May Sarton. Chief among them was Josephine Hutchinson (daughter of Leona Roberts, best remembered as Mrs. Meade in *Gone with the Wind*), who received excellent notices as Wendy in *Peter Pan* and as Alice in *Alice in Wonderland*. It was during an interview with Kathy Nolan—Wendy to Mary Martin's Peter Pan in the original Broadway run and two "live" telecasts—that Nolan casually mentioned that she brunched weekly with "the other Wendy."

"And who is that?" I asked politely, not expecting to hear a reply that would prove of any interest to me.

"Josie," she answered nonchalantly.

"Josie?" I perked up. "Is that short for…"

"Josephine Hutchinson! Have you interviewed her yet?"

"Interviewed her?" I yelped with excitement. "I had no idea that she was alive! For the last year I've been desperately trying to obtain an interview with Eva Le Gallienne. I never thought of Josephine Hutchinson."

"Josie lives upstairs. Would you like to meet her?" Nolan asked impishly even as she wrote down her address. "Now, she has very poor eyesight, so your writing will need to be very large."

I typed a letter on my old typewriter—this was before computers—and photocopied it to be as large as possible. A week later I received a lovely letter from Miss Hutchinson in which she expressed her joy in playing Wendy:

> 360 East 55th St.
> New York, N.Y. 10022
> March 13, 1990

Dear Mr. Hanson,

It pleases me that Kathy Nolan has given you my address because your research project sounds most interesting, and I would be willing to talk about Peter Pan since I thoroughly enjoyed playing Wendy. It is one of my favorites, and I have a number of charming and amusing anecdotes from the live performances that you may wish to use in your book.

Since you teach, I imagine your week is rather busy with professional duties and that Saturdays would be the best days for you to come into Manhattan for interviews. Saturdays would be most convenient for me also. Come and have a cup of tea with me while we talk about Peter Pan.

If you will telephone me at your convenience any morning until noon (I'm an early riser), or any afternoon after 3:00 p.m., I'll be glad to make a mutually convenient time for us to meet. My unlisted telephone number is…

I shall look forward to meeting you and discussing your work on Peter Pan.

Sincerely Yours,
Josephine Hutchinson

I was dialing her number before I even finished reading the letter. A few minutes later we made an appointment to meet at her penthouse apartment on the Upper East Side just a floor above Kathy Nolan's residence. As I had done with others I had interviewed, I threw a piece of pottery on my wheel as a thank-you gift—this time, a teapot for our tea party. Armed with my tape recorder, a legal pad, pencils, and my carefully wrapped teapot, I drove into Manhattan with much anticipation. Miss Hutchinson answered the door herself and immediately apologized for her poor eyesight and for using a handkerchief to wipe her mouth, as she would occasionally drool. She opened her present like a child on Christmas morning and then, after expressing excitement over her new teapot, asked me if I might prepare the tea. However, even with her poor eyesight she detected my clumsy attempt to brew the tea with loose tea leaves. She boomed regally, "You don't drink tea, do you?"

"Not really," I admitted sheepishly. *That's it! I've lost everything. She is going to end our interview right now!*

"Why did you agree to tea then?"

"I would have said yes to coffee, beer, or a martini if you had asked. I don't like any of them either, but I would drink them to interview you. I'm afraid I don't like most adult beverages."

"Well, then," she responded with a chuckle, "I had better prepare the tea. And please, call me Josie." I helped bring out a tray with teacups, saucers, biscuits, raspberry tea, cream, sugar cubes, and my teapot. What was scheduled to be a twenty-minute interview turned into a three-and-a-half-hour joy ride as Josie not only answered my questions but went into very detailed accounts of the preparation of *Peter Pan* at the Civic Repertory Theatre. We digressed a few times as she shed light on her stage and screen career as well as her special friendship with LeG. Somehow, we got to the subject of Alfred Hitchcock, for whom she appeared as James Mason's wife in *North by Northwest*. She explained that Hitchcock was very cheap and decided to save money by not using her later in the film. However, he still needed to imply her presence, so he asked Josie's husband if he could borrow the dress she had worn, since it was hers. Quite angry with the master director to begin with, she refused, and in the end, her character in the film simply disappears.

We also discussed at some length her romantic relationship with Eva Le Gallienne. I was surprised to learn that she was present in Le Gallienne's Connecticut home when LeG was caught in an explosion in the basement. Eva was badly burned, but in her autobiographies omitted Josephine's presence, probably to protect Josephine's reputation even though she had already been labeled by the press as Le Gallienne's *shadow*, a term used for lesbian. Despite a sad end to their relationship, they remained friends until the end of Le Gallienne's life, although Josephine wed two more times. (She was married to Robert W. Bell, the son of Alexander Graham Bell, when the relationship began.) Interestingly, her career was never hurt by her well-known affair with Le Gallienne. Years later she was open with the press, saying, "It's quite natural for actors to fall in love with the people they work with. It was good and normal and healthy. There was never any sense of shame connected with our relationship."

Of greater interest to me at the time were her connections with *Peter Pan* and *Alice in Wonderland*. The first performance of *Alice* took place one evening when Le Gallienne, realizing there was not enough time to strike the sets used during rehearsal to prepare for the evening showing of *Peter Pan*, asked the audience if they wouldn't mind having a sneak preview. They responded enthusiastically as the critics and audiences did later after the play officially opened. So popular was *Alice in Wonderland* at the Civic Repertory Theatre on Fourteenth Street that it moved to the New Amsterdam Theatre nearly a month later on January 30, 1933. It was revived on Broadway again on April 5, 1947, where it played for one hundred performances at the Majestic Theatre with LeG again playing the White Queen, and yet again in 1971 but with disastrous results. Suddenly, Josie walked over to a bookcase and pulled out a six 78 rpm record set of *Alice*. "Are you familiar with this recording?" she asked.

"Yes, indeed! I've been looking for that set for several years. The twelve-inch records have never been reissued in any other format." It was the RCA Broadway cast album produced in 1947 with selections from Richard Addinsell's whimsical score as well as dialogue and songs performed by Eva Le Gallienne as the Narrator and the White Chess Queen, Margaret Webster as the Cheshire Cat and the Red Chess Queen, William Windom as the White Rabbit, Henry Jones as the Mouse, Eli Wallach as the Duck and Knave of Hearts, and Bambi Linn as Alice: quite a stellar cast!

The 1947 Broadway cast of *Alice in Wonderland and Through the Looking Glass* was recorded on six 78 rpm records but has never been officially reissued. Unfortunately, the earlier version with Josephine Hutchinson was not recorded. RCA K-13

Reading my mind, she smiled and asked, "Would you like to borrow it?"

"Borrow it? I'd love to! I could record it and have it back to you by next week."

"That would be fine," she remarked calmly. "I am downsizing my apartment and will be donating the records along with other theater memorabilia to the Lincoln Center Theater library." I left her apartment late that afternoon with my cassettes, recorder, legal pad, and *Alice* record album safely tucked under my arm. A few days later, Josie called me to make certain that I was returning the record set that weekend. I drove to her penthouse once more and, after a few polite niceties, rode the elevator down while thinking about her records. Suddenly I remembered that the library already had *Alice in Wonderland* in its collection and that it would probably show up in their annual white elephant sale. I was a volunteer for that event, so perhaps, I thought, just perhaps I could buy it.

The Sunday event took place just a few months after my interview with Josie. On the main floor of the library, I found several scrapbooks and magazines relating to Maude Adams, the first Peter Pan in the United States. During my break, I asked one of the organizers if there were any 78 rpm records for sale. He told me that they had decided to omit 78s because they were losing popularity at the sales, and were too heavy and fragile for them to move about. However, he directed me to the basement, where records in other formats were being sold. Disappointed with his reply, I decided to look anyway. The small room was set up with tables against the walls, each with four or five boxes of records. One box in particular seemed to be crowded with large record sets. Ignoring the other boxes, I went straight for that one, and lo and behold, Josie's record set was in the middle, marked with a red elephant sticker. I held it in my hand as tears filled my eyes—not because I was thrilled to be able to buy those records, as indeed I was, but because Josie's beloved treasure could be obtained for a mere two dollars. Then, a practical voice from inside whispered that it was still a treasure, but this time, it was mine. I still own it and listen to it every Christmas season just as we watch *The Homecoming: A Christmas Story*, the very first *Waltons* television movie, in which Josie played Mamie Baldwin opposite Dorothy Stickney's

Emily Baldwin, the elderly rich spinsters who made "Papa's Recipe," their own bootleg liquor.

Alice in Wonderland was never reissued by RCA but was restored from original 78s in the Belfer Archive of Syracuse University by Alan Bunting for Must Close Saturday Records in 2004. The recording still holds up, so if you are an *Alice* fan (and who isn't?), please look on eBay, where it is occasionally listed. Meticulously restored, the sixty-odd-minute CD has only one problem: the beautiful RCA album cover was replaced by a John Tenniel drawing. Lovely as it is, the original *Alice* illustration lacks the theatricality of the jacket featuring Bambi Linn and other Tenniel illustrations. No problem! I simply made a reduced copy of the RCA album and inserted it over the existing one. It reminds me of my teenage days when I made homemade cover art for my cassette soundtracks that I recorded directly from my television. But even more, it reminds me of Josephine Hutchinson.

Alice in Wonderland remains one of my most cherished albums. I listened to it while writing this chapter and cried when I reread Josie's letter to me. She may have died in 1998 at the age of ninety-four, but she comes alive whenever I look at *Peter Pan* photos, *The Homecoming: A Christmas Story*, and, of course, when I revisit *Alice*.

CHAPTER 18

Skyscraper

Spare that building, don't tear it down
Spare that building, it has renown

—SAMMY CAHN AND JIMMY VAN HEUSEN

LIKE MANY PARENTS RAISING THEIR first child, Donna and I went through many trials and tribulations until we felt, correctly or not, that we were doing the right thing. We were determined that we would have supper each night as a family and dine rather than gulp down our meals. After dessert and coffee, my son, Drew, would ask to be excused from the kitchen table so he could play with his building blocks on the floor nearby.

One evening, as his mother and I were in deep conversation, one of Drew's architectural wonders collapsed, to which he quickly responded, "Shit!" Donna and I stared at each other. Had we really heard our three-year-old say "shit"? No, it couldn't be. But a few minutes later another building fell and again Drew muttered, "Shit."

"Drew!" Donna jumped at him. "Where did you learn that?"

"Grammy Bones," he replied nonchalantly, referring to his grandmother.

"When does Grammy Bones say that?" I asked.

"Whenever she loses in cards." Donna's mother watched Drew during the day while we worked, but that did not prevent her from hosting her once-a-week poker games.

"Well, you cannot ever say that word again, Drew."

"Why, Daddy?"

"Because it's a very bad word. Do you understand? Never again!"

"Okay, Daddy," he answered agreeably. Donna and I resumed our conversation as Drew built yet another structure with his building blocks. Then, like the others, it fell. Donna and I looked at Drew and smiled, because obviously he had learned his lesson.

"Son of a bitch!" he exclaimed.

The 1965 Broadway cast recording of *Skyscraper* with Julie Harris. During the 1974 Tony Award telecast, Charles Nelson Reilly stopped the show with his comic routine about being on stage performing mediocre songs but being off-stage changing his costume while the stars performed the hits of the show. His version of "Spare That Building" from *Skyscraper* was hilarious. Capitol VAS 2422

CHAPTER 19

From Russia with Love

From Russia with love I fly to you,
Much wiser since my good-bye to you

—LIONEL BART

FOR THREE YEARS THE HIGH school where I taught enjoyed an exchange program with students and instructors from Russia, and I was fortunate to have been chosen by my friend Judy to chaperone our students in Russia as well as sponsor a Russian teacher in my home in North Carolina. On weekends, we would take field trips to D.C. and Busch Gardens. One day in school, while all of our students were taking PSAT tests, I volunteered to take our Russian friends to my art room where I would teach them some theater games. One in particular, I thought, would be helpful with their English. I have no name for it, but it goes like this:

The students create a new language by saying a word, demonstrating it through charades, and then writing it phonetically on the board. As each word is introduced, the group imitates the actions of the creator and then repeats the word as they physically mime the meaning. Then, after everyone in the group has had an opportunity to do their presentation, they are broken into smaller groups to create an original scene using only the new vocabulary. As an example, I might use an onomatopoeic word such as "slurp" while holding an imaginary straw to my mouth, and the group knows that I mean "to drink." Complicated? No—or at least I thought not.

Everything was going well until one Russian boy stood up to teach us his word. He clapped his hands loudly and said, Pu-see!" At once everyone else in the class, the teachers and other students from Russia stood up and applauded with the same gusto. "Pu-see! Pu-see!" I started to panic and looked around to make sure that no one else in the hall or next rooms heard them. No one. Good. This little vocabulary lesson would go no further than my room. After the groups improvised and presented their scenes, class was dismissed, and that was that. Or so I thought...

The soundtrack album of the 1963 James Bond film,
From Russia with Love. United Artists UAL 4114

That night the Russians and their American hosts went to a school football game, but I was not available to help chaperone. However, two nights later I joined them at a local bowling alley. A non-athlete who throws a baseball like a girl, I am absolutely hopeless on a bowling lane. When my son, Drew, was younger, it was always a challenge as I tried to teach him to bowl.

In the years since, I had not improved, and told everyone that night I would just watch.

"No, no, no!" my Russian friend Marina insisted. "You must play just like us. We do not know bowling too!" Rolling my eyes as far back as I could, I agreed and picked up a ball. As I approached the line on the lane, all of the Russians stood up, clapped loudly, and yelled, "Mr. Hanson: pu-see, pu-see!" I couldn't believe my ears. I quickly turned around to shush them but they only repeated more loudly, "Mr. Hanson: pu-see!" The ball was thrown and ended up in the gutter before it had rolled even halfway down the lane.

"Better luck next time," Marina shouted. A few minutes later it was my turn again, and just as before, I was greeted with the loudest cheers ever heard in a bowling alley, not only from the Russians but from my own students as well. "MR. HANSON! PU-SEE, PU-SEE!"

Suddenly Judy came out of nowhere, grabbed me by the collar, and asked, "They're calling you a pussy! Why are they calling you a pussy?"

"It's, it's a misunderstanding!" I exclaimed, short of breath. "We played the phonetics game, and they think *pussy* means 'to clap.'" I elaborated, "It's not *pussy* they're saying, it's P-U-S-E-E!"

"Oh, well, that makes total sense," she replied as she loosened the grip on my neck.

"Why is that?" I asked, gasping for breath.

"Two nights ago during the football game our star quarterback was racing across the field and the crowd was cheering but the Russians were clapping and shouting at him, 'Pussy! Pussy!'"

CHAPTER 20

Pillow Talk

Wonder how it would be to have
Someone to pillow talk with me

—BUDDY PEPPER AND INEZ JAMES

WHENEVER I GO AWAY ON a trip for school or research, my partner, Dale, sees to it that I come home to a surprise, which could be anything from rearranging furniture to painting a room. In addition, he likes to play practical jokes on me. For example, I noticed immediately upon returning from New Mexico that he had painted the bedroom, but it took a few minutes to find a giant stuffed black widow spider sitting on the toilet. Another time, he bought new bedroom sheets and a comforter, but he also wallpapered the bathroom. However, he outdid himself when I traveled with my students to Russia, where I was to teach visual arts and theater to children of various ages in the Komi Republic.

On the morning of my departure it was snowing in North Carolina, where we lived at the time. Dale was hurrying me, as the early morning two-hour drive to the Norfolk, Virginia, airport would be treacherous and take more time. He suggested that I take along my favorite pillow, which we often laughingly referred to as Pillow Boy, since I am a rather restless sleeper without it. But with the airline weight and luggage restrictions, not to mention the desire to maintain a bit of dignity in front of my students, I decided it was a bad idea.

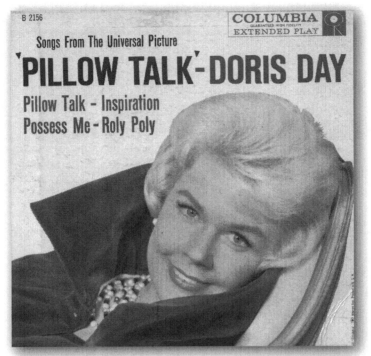

The best-selling 45 rpm single of *Pillow Talk* by Doris Day.
The film compelled Oscar Levan to proclaim that he knew
Doris Day before she was virgin. Columbia B 2156

We arrived at the airport minutes before loading time, much to the relief
of my friend Judy, who was the coordinator of the trip and the only other
adult chaperone for the twelve or so students. "Glad you could make it," she
murmured to me wryly out of the side of her mouth.

"You won't believe this, but we woke up to snow in North Carolina!"
I defended myself. I hugged Dale, who was about to drive back home, and
whispered in his ear, "Don't abuse Pillow Boy. Don't sleep with him."

The flight to Russia was a trip unto itself. When we reached Moscow, our
luggage was wrapped in several layers of thick, clear tape so it would not be
broken into during the changing of planes to Syktyvkar, which was still about
four hundred miles away. We landed on a runway thick with compressed snow
and ice and were met in the lobby by extremely aggressive taxi drivers flirting

with our female students. After several hours we boarded a frighteningly small aircraft for the shakiest flight I had ever experienced, arriving at our destination around three in the morning. Our reception was amazing, though, with our Russian students and their families cheering us with homemade welcome signs outside the tiny airport.

My hosts were the family of a third-grade Russian teacher named Marina who gave up their living room for my quarters. The building they lived in—indeed, most of the buildings in which the Russian families resided—was unimaginatively designed and constructed in the sixties of concrete, appearing more like a fortress than an apartment building. There were no foyers, and the hallways and small elevators were dimly lighted and quite dreary, with heavily bundled young men hanging out, openly drinking vodka from bottles. Because there was practically no heat in these hallways, the image conveyed was rather threatening. Marina's flat had two doors; the first was a heavily bolted, metal dungeon-like door, which, when opened, revealed a lovely wooden door that was highly polished. Inside, the contrast was amazing! It was toasty warm with wall-to-wall carpeting, fancy throw rugs hung on the walls like tapestries, and various styles of tiles that conflicted with each other as well as with my sense of design. Marina's two boys were still sleeping, so I was led to the living room, where I would be residing over the next three weeks.

The next morning, I was greeted by Sasha, a mischievous cat who hid under my convertible couch and attacked my bare feet. I quickly learned to wear heavy wool socks wherever I walked in the flat. Marina's boys and her husband were waiting for me in the kitchen with an American breakfast and cold fruit juices that Marina thoughtfully remembered as my favorite part of a meal. As her husband did not speak English, nor I Russian, Marina and her eldest son became my interpreters. We hurried through our meal because we were going to school that same morning, and even though I was exhausted from the flight the night before, the exhilaration over what was in store provided the adrenaline I needed for the next fourteen hours.

That first morning—indeed, almost every morning—we Americans were bombarded with students and teachers who wanted to meet with us and wanted us to sign their notebooks. It was as if we were celebrities or important dignitaries. Every night except the two when Judy and I prepared dinners, we dined with a different family, each approaching the event as an honor to feed us. Our hosting families took note of our likings, and I soon found caviar, cream cheese, smoked salmon, and black bread at practically every supper. We ate lunches in the school cafeteria where our students were waited on hand and foot. These meals, different from those served to the main student body, usually consisted of cold tomato and salmon salads, bread, various types of borscht, meats and fish, and a fruit beverage concocted from local berries. Often the salads would either be accented only with salt and pepper or the most delicious mayonnaise I have ever tasted in my life—more like a sour cream.

Initially, I attended a couple of extremely boring art classes where the students merely copied various patterns that were prevalent in Syktyvkar culture. Judy defended the art teacher, who was trying to preserve their artistic traditions in a modern world. In order not to insult the art teacher, we decided that I would teach acting classes, which were not available in their school. Judy, a jack-of-all-trades, taught various teaching methods to the other teachers that were enthusiastically received. The school was heavily heated; we entered bundled up for their icy winter only to strip down to jeans and shirts once inside.

The school was the center of the students' educational and social lives; thus we had classes even on Saturdays. It was open most evenings as well, and the kids attended dances, worked on craft projects, or merely hung out. Between classes the hallways were crowded, but as soon as the next scheduled class was to commence, the halls emptied quickly without any prodding from the teachers. This was quite different from what I was used to in my school back home, where we practically had to drag our students out of the hallways after the bell had rung. In fact, I can't remember the Russians using bells at all.

With the exception of Sundays, when we went sightseeing, most of our days were spent in school or at the gymnasium, where one of the student's fathers was in charge. Because organized religion had been banned from their parents' lives in the forties and fifties, there was not much in terms of rituals.

Yes, there was a Russian Orthodox church, but most of the people in the community treated it more like a historical relic than a place of worship. In fact, Christmas was hardly celebrated. Instead, January was the time to exchange presents and welcome a visit from Father New Year. Although I was not religious myself, seeing how public expressions of faith had been forcefully removed from their lives filled me with pride in my own country and great sorrow for the people of Russia. Many of the beautiful architectural turrets of Moscow had been strategically demolished by the Communists in an attempt to eliminate outward signs of religious worship.

One weekend we were treated to a holiday getaway at a communal-type hotel that sponsored games, skiing, sleigh riding, and dances at night. During the Saturday night dance, the other teachers, all women, decided that they would have a tea party in their room while I chaperoned our students at the dance. I was a bit apprehensive about being left alone, because the dance was attended by many patrons of the hotel who were strangers, but I danced with my students and managed to enjoy myself. Then, out of nowhere, a rather unattractive and extremely drunk middle-aged woman cut in and insisted that I dance with her. In vain, but much to the delight of my students—Russian and American—I tried to explain that I was a teacher and really needed to be watching them. However, this did not deter the woman from her mission. Trying my best not to create a scene, I found myself dancing with her for twenty minutes or so. Even without a translator, it was obvious that I was being invited to her room. Thankfully, Katie, one of my theater students, went upstairs to the tea party to ask the other teachers to "rescue" me.

Judy and the Russian teachers walked into the dance in a pack, and one of them, an extremely attractive redhead, broke into our dance, grabbing me and saying to the drunken woman in Russian, "He's mine!" The woman retreated to her room alone. After that, the rest of the evening was uneventful, although a young man also tried in vain to persuade me to go to his room.

Another weekend we were all invited to a vacation cabin of the hosting families. During the day the male Russian students persuaded me, along with my students, to go into a sauna in our swimming trunks where we lay on wooden benches as they lightly hit our backs, legs, and arms with white birch tree branches. This traditional ritual has the recipient becoming too hot to stay in the sauna, running outside in only a bathing suit, and diving into a bank of snow. Of course, my students wanted me to do this as well, and I received cheers worthy of some heroic effort when I complied. Judy caught the act on camera and later included it on a bulletin board display in her school office.

That night several of us gathered in a circle and played a game of improvisation with an endless story where each person added a line. Monsters and all sorts of supernatural antagonists could not destroy our fictitious hero, who was always miraculously brought back to life by one participant after another one had killed him off. We drank the berry drink and stuffed ourselves with a barbecue-like beef roasted on an open flame. It was here that I leaned how the annual berry and mushroom gatherings in the summers kept the residents of Syktyvkar from starving during the fall of the Soviet Union. Inside every flat, hidden behind the walls, were rows and rows of shelves filled with bottles of the berry drink, mushrooms, and vegetables that they had canned during the summers to be served as treats during the long winter months. No one would have suspected that these provisions would be their lifeline.

One of the most memorable visits for me was at the flat of Marina's sister and her husband, where I met their parents. The father was a small round man, warm and funny, with whom I conversed for hours thanks to his daughter's translation skills. He asked as many questions about my home in the States as I did about his. Particularly, I remember a poignant conversation about his experiences as a boy during World War II: the cruelty of the German army when they invaded Russia and his fears for his family as well as himself. Being Jewish I could comprehend even more and we bonded in many ways. I shall never forget the loving quality of his family and the people of Syktyvkar in general.

Three weeks later, we left the Komi Republic in tears as we realized that we would probably never see these people again. For the remainder of our trip, we stayed in a hotel in Moscow that had been built the year they hosted the Olympics decades earlier. Quite dated, it had several prostitutes "working" in the lobby who were dated themselves. My students and I were amazed at their blatant sexuality and their tacky but revealing attire.

It was much warmer in Moscow than in Syktyvkar—about twenty degrees Fahrenheit—so we spent most of our days outside exploring Red Square and buying souvenirs from the many outside vendors who were quite willing to bargain with us for their Russian dolls and other trinkets. Lined along the streets were statues of famous Russian artists and writers. It was near a sculpture of Anton Chekov that a few of my students and I were approached by an elderly man with white hair and a long beard who began telling us a story about this particular street. His English was quite clear, and he was very entertaining. After another story or two, he explained that he had a very small pension and that he supplemented it by selling his stories, reminding me of a character from the musical *Kismet*. My students artfully walked away, but I stayed to listen to more. After twenty minutes, I asked his name, to which he replied, "Sam."

"Sam…" I quietly asked, "are you a Samuel?" Staring at me for some time with great caution, he finally said, "Call me a schmuck, but I am a Jew in Russia." I confessed to him that I too was Jewish, which perhaps he sensed, and that I was thankful for his oral tradition of storytelling. I dug into my pocket and pulled out my wallet. "How much do I owe you?" Not at all embarrassed, he smiled and said 634 rubles, which was about $10. Instead, I handed him the equivalent of $200. Please understand that I am not independently wealthy; I just thought I would bring home fewer trinkets.

We flew back home to Norfolk, where there was a snowstorm that caused Dale to be very late in picking me up. On the ride home the local radio station announced that schools would be closed the next day, which was fine with me, since all I wanted to do was sleep. Because I knew something would be different in the house, I looked around: an antique chair and rocker had been added to the living room. Dale had removed them from storage. Otherwise, everything else was just as I had left it.

Before going to bed I phoned my parents in California. My mother answered the phone as usual: breathless as though she had just run a marathon. She asked me if I was able to trace any of her family from Russia, reminding me that her maiden name, Tatarsky, ended with a *y* and not an *i*. I explained that the Russian alphabet was quite different from ours and it would have been impossible in the limited time I was there. However, I did tell her about Samuel the Storyteller, and with much pride, bragged about giving him $200. "Did you take his address?" Mom asked.

"Why would I do that?" I asked a little defensively.

"So you could send him more money during the year."

After a few more minutes I told Mom that I was exhausted and desperately needed sleep. I finally walked into the bedroom. I couldn't believe what I was seeing! Pillow Boy, my favorite pillow, was on the mattress, with each corner tied to a bedpost. Gray duct tape crisscrossed over his imaginary mouth, and a few inches away, a small mirror was laced with two rows of flour and a razor blade. Beside them was a VHS videotape labeled *"XXX—Pillow Boy: He Delivers."*

CHAPTER 21

Annie Get Your Gun

Anything you can sing I can sing better
I can sing anything better than you

—IRVING BERLIN

INEVITABLY, ONE OF THE QUESTIONS musical comedy aficionados are confronted with is this: *Gypsy*—Ethel, Patti, Angela, Bernadette, or Rosalind? I allowed my theater class to take a crack at this and Patti LuPone won. Of course, I could only play excerpts of pirate videos and recordings for them, so this survey wasn't exactly based on science. My friend Robert Gable saw the great Merm in the original run, and until he died he swore no one played it better. Raymond Wood, another friend, could not find enough adjectives to express the effect Angela Lansbury had on him in the role in the early seventies. I think it's a shame that Rosalind Russell won the role over Judy Garland, who not only performed the most dynamic version of "Some People" in her concerts but also most likely would have understood Momma Rose, because her mother, Ethel Gumm, was almost as notorious a backstage mother as Gypsy Rose Lee's. In fact, Stephen Sondheim and Jule Styne expressed great interest in Garland playing the role, but one of the producers was Russell's husband.

If I had to choose the definitive recording, it would be quite difficult, because I grew up with the film soundtrack and still enjoy the singing of Lisa

Kirk, who, incidentally, dubbed for Rosalind Russell. Then there is Angela Lansbury's British import, and although she was not quite up to the vocals of Ethel Merman, she did capture the monstrous quality of Momma Rose. I also enjoy the vocal selections featuring Natalie Wood and Ann Jillian as Louise and Dainty June on the film soundtrack.

The first pressing of the MGM soundtrack of
Annie Get Your Gun on the 78 rpm format with
Betty Hutton and Howard Keel. MGM 50

Coincidentally, the other leading question involves Annie—Annie Oakley—in Irving Berlin's *Annie Get Your Gun*. Who was better? Again, Mr. Gable saw Ethel Merman originate the role and insisted that she was best. My niece Jessie was just as strong in her opinion of Bernadette Peters. I played a couple of the sequences from the aborted film version starring Judy Garland along with the entire film with Betty Hutton for my friend Steven, a professional wig maker, and he preferred Betty. Barbara Cook went gaga

over Reba McIntire when she replaced Bernadette Peters in the very success-
ful Broadway revival.

What about yours truly? In terms of the film and television performances I prefer Betty Hutton. Mind you, there are issues with her portrayal, the
biggest being that Betty was way over the top in the emotional scenes. But
she was exceptional in her comic delivery, and the up-tempo numbers were
fun, frothy, and often hysterically funny, especially "I've Got the Sun in the
Morning" as well as her duet with Howard Keel of "Anything You Can Do."
But her handling of the ballads was weak—very weak.

On the other hand, in her few scenes Judy Garland approached Annie in a
more realistic manner but lacked the necessary humor, which is understandable,
considering how sick she was and that she would soon be removed from the film
altogether. On the soundtrack her songs drag, especially "You Can't Get a Man
with a Gun," which is not given as fast a tempo as Hutton's. Yet when she sings
"Let's Go West Again," not one of Berlin's best songs, one wishes that MGM
would have given her a few months off before the pre-recordings as well as the
actual filming, especially when you consider that the revamped *Annie* began
production at the same time that Judy commenced work on *Summer Stock*.
Her voice here is lovely, soft, and full, expressing the vulnerability that Betty
never was able to conjure up. It is rather ironic then that *Annie Get Your Gun*,
although a fun film, is not the classic musical film it should have been, whereas
Judy's performance of "Get Happy" in *Summer Stock*, the film she was shoved
into after losing *Annie*, somehow emerges as an almost quintessential backstage
musical with a classic performance by Garland.

Which recorded versions do I listen to most? Thank you for asking; this is
the order of my preferences: Betty Hutton, Mary Martin, Judy Garland, Ethel
Merman (the Decca version), Ethel Merman (the RCA version), Dolores Gray,
Doris Day, and Bernadette Peters. Sorry, Jessie!

Judy Garland in a costume test for the film version of Annie *Get Your Gun*. She was replaced by Betty Hutton. Garland's 1949 *Annie* recordings were sold for many years on pirate albums until the Rhino label issued them all on CD in 2000.

CHAPTER 22

Good Times

And the beat goes on
And the beat goes on

—Sonny Bono

Did you see *Good Times* with Sonny and Cher? I thought not. I bought a sealed copy of the vinyl soundtrack a few months ago in an attempt to build on my existing soundtrack collection, but upon one playback it left me with little desire to ever see the film. Actually, perhaps I am being a little strong here; it left me with a feeling of great indifference, if indifference can indeed be great. This was unusual for me because I am quite opinionated, as if you didn't know that by now.

Over the years since eBay has grown, I have watched my beloved record collection decline in value. Yes, the real value of collecting is the pleasure it brings to the collector, not the worth of the collection. And I do acknowledge that my records provide great comfort in their intrinsic purpose: listening pleasure. Still, it would be even more comforting to know that my records were worth more than or at least the same as they were in 1990. That would also bring me great comfort.

Then there is my job. Although I adore teaching and working with kids, there is often a feeling of futility in trying to help students who aren't in-terested in art or theater or school for that matter. Why is it that I take it personally when a student of mine is turned off to pottery, painting or acting? More importantly, what can I do to engage that student when he or she hardly comes to school?

The soundtrack of the 1967 film *Good Times* with Sonny and Cher. Atco 33-214

Take Cathy, for example: she was smart and attractive, although not particularly well liked by her peers. Sadly, I wondered if anyone really was affected by her school attendance. She came to school only when the possibility of being arrested for truancy threatened her world. To be fair, Cathy's existence looked as bleak as Andrew Wyeth's *Christina's World*. Her father was in prison for some undisclosed crime and her mother was a crackhead. At the time she was my student, Cathy had been sleeping on and off with a twenty-five-year-old loser. Did I mention that Cathy was only fifteen years old? She was an on-again, off-again runaway, and it was my other students, Cathy's grandmother, and Facebook who kept me abreast of her whereabouts and well-being. Out of school for several months living with her boyfriend, she came back only when a judge threatened to lock her up in a juvenile detention center.

Once, when Cathy made one of her occasional appearances, I called her grandmother to see if she had also come back home. "No," she murmured, "but will you please tell her that I love her and miss her and want her home again?"

Her truancy officer told me that although the teenager liked me and my class, she had no intentions of working. "The judge told me I had to go to school," she bragged to her case manager. "He didn't say anything about me having to work."

"But why waste your time?" I asked. "Why waste the whole year?"

"I'll do the work next year," was her simple but unrealistic reply.

Now, I do not allow students to just sit and converse in my classes, so there were several occasions when Cathy was not working that I would send her to another classroom to be with students outside her comfort level. However, when it soon became obvious that this was not working, I decided I had to be bold, to catch Cathy alone and share some events of my life that perhaps she could relate to. The wait was not long. After not showing up to my class for several days, she suddenly made an entrance and sat and played with clay. A short time later she raised her hand and asked if she could have a pass to go to the restroom.

"Sure thing," I answered, beckoning her to my desk. "Sit down for a second while I fill out the pass." Because she was sitting near me, I took advantage of the moment. "Cathy, I'm going to share something with you. I know that you know that I know [*shit, what a way to hook her*] about your parents. I want you to know that I can empathize with you. My father was an extremely abusive man who beat my mother with whatever he could, once even with a vacuum cleaner. I can remember when my brother and I were so afraid of him that we hid under our beds. I was sure he was going to kill us. When my parents divorced, he was supposed to take us back to Michigan to arrange for the moving of our furniture and stuff back to New York. I was only ten years old at the time. But instead, he never returned us to my mother. He kept us with him for about three months and then dumped us off at his mother's in Minnesota. We didn't see my mother for over a year.

"This next thing is something I've never told a living soul. As a child, because I was so frightened of my father, and because I hated him so much, I was sure that I was gay only because I didn't want to be like him. I didn't know then that homosexuality was an inherited gene. Of course I eventually found out that the fear of my father had nothing to do with my sexuality."

I had to fight back the tears while Cathy stared at me with a blank expression. "The point is," I continued, "the point is that I was only ten, but I knew that I was going to overcome this handicap and do what I wanted to do. I was going to become an artist. Do you understand what I am trying to tell you?"

There was a brief moment of quiet and for me, a moment of hope that maybe, just maybe, I had reached Cathy by spilling my guts out. "Mr. Hanson," she finally said with indifference, "I just want to go to the bathroom."

Maybe I need to give *Good Times* another play on the turntable. "The Beat Goes On."

CHAPTER 23

The Unsinkable
Molly Brown

But till I leave the rear
It's from the rear you'll hear
I ain't down yet.

—MEREDITH WILSON

I WAS A BIT APPREHENSIVE about writing this chapter because suddenly it's popular to write glowing testimonials about Debbie Reynolds, but ask any of my friends and you'll find out that I have been a fan of her work since I was a kid. She is a natural comedienne, a dynamic singer and dancer, and for many years was the most wholesome girl on the silver screen. She can boast being a star in perhaps the best original musical comedy in motion picture history, *Singin' in the Rain*. Her performance in Albert Brooks' film *Mother* was perfection, and shame on the Academy Awards for overlooking that performance. The film was almost perfect too except for the instant happy ending where Brooks meets a very attractive woman. In many ways, Debbie Reynolds's career has been overlooked but never more than during the 1965 Oscars, when she lost the statue to Julie Andrews.

Debbie Reynolds as Molly Brown seemed to bounce right off the screen in 1964. Here she is seen performing "I Ain't Down Yet."

There is no argument that Julie Andrews gave a remarkably fresh and lovely performance in *Mary Poppins*, certainly good enough to be nominated for the many awards she received that year. Yet I can't help thinking that part of those awards was demonstrative venting by industry insiders because of their extreme dislike of Harry Warner, who unforgivably cast Audrey Hepburn as Eliza Doolittle instead of Andrews, who created the role on Broadway. Today it's almost impossible to conceive of such an act, but even in 1962 Julie Andrews was popular enough through her television special with Carol Burnett and the earlier musical adaptation of *Cinderella* by Rodgers and Hammerstein to have been a serious contender for the film. Added to this was her definitive portrayal of Eliza in *My Fair Lady* on Broadway and in London, not to mention the lovely and haunting *Camelot* with Richard Burton. But Harry Warner wanted a superstar, which is what he got with Audrey Hepburn.

Julie Andrews was nominated again in 1966 for her stunning portrayal of Maria von Trapp in *The Sound of Music* for what could easily have been the most saccharine role of all time. Instead, and with much aid from Christopher Plummer, she turned a cardboard character into real and likable flesh and blood. Andrews should have received the Oscar that year, but another Julie— Julie Christie—won instead. As for her Oscar-winning performance in *Mary Poppins*, I think Carrie Fisher expresses it best in a very funny book and film, *Wishful Drinking*, which she says her mother, Debbie Reynolds, lost to Julie Andrews's Method acting. Fisher clearly loves her mother, but she is also painfully honest about her.

Then there is Audrey Hepburn, who later apologized to Andrews for accepting the lead in the screen adaptation of *My Fair Lady*. "I couldn't help myself," she told her (or something along that line). Of course she couldn't! I wouldn't have turned it down either! To work with George Cukor, not to mention the musical director André Previn, was a dream come true. And perhaps, had the artistic team rethought the vocals for Hepburn, it might have worked out. But instead, the musical arrangements were maintained for a singer of Andrews's stature, leaving poor Audrey to sing songs outside her range. No wonder she was hurt when she was told that her vocals would be dubbed. She was so wounded and angry that she did not show up to work after the announcements were made public. I would not have gone to work that day either.

Marni Nixon is the voice we hear on most of Audrey's musical moments on-screen, but with mixed results. Nothing against Miss Nixon, who was a fine singer, but when Audrey opens her mouth to sing and we hear Marni instead, it is fairly obvious that the voice is dubbed. Much of it has to do with the placement of the mouth and throat. Audrey was not a trained singer, so she does not look like she is singing those soaring notes of "I Could Have Danced All Night." Marni operated best with Deborah Kerr in the film version of *The King and I* because the two performers worked together rather than Marni coming in later to fix the problem, as she also did when she covered for Natalie Wood in *West Side Story*. *Why does Hollywood insist on casting non-singers in great singing roles?* You actually believe Deborah Kerr is singing. Incidentally, Kerr was nominated for an Oscar for her performance.

Despite my misgivings about her vocals, I believe that Audrey Hepburn gave the best acting performance in a musical of 1964. Of the three noted musical films, *My Fair Lady* holds up best, especially in the scenes between Rex Harrison's Professor Higgins and Audrey Hepburn's Eliza Doolittle. I watch the movie several times a year. However, the Academy Award for the female lead, although often cited as the Best Actress Award, is actually presented each year as the award to the actress who gave the best performance in a film. Not best actress, mind you, but best performance.

Therefore, it is my firm belief that Debbie Reynolds should have won the Oscar, for not only is her portrayal of Molly Brown rich in detail, pathos, and comedy, but she also sang her own songs with a gusto not seen before in a screen musical and danced to extremely difficult choreography, far more than Julie Andrews in *Mary Poppins*. Like an Eliza Doolittle, she transforms herself from a poor country girl to the sophisticated lady who saves the lives of fellow passengers on the *Titanic*. Molly Brown was the role of a lifetime, and Reynolds recognized that when she saw the play on Broadway. And who would have ever thought that over fifty years later Debbie Reynolds would still be wowing audiences with her exuberance and acting skills.

The Unsinkable Molly Brown is one of my favorite soundtrack albums. Its only fault is that there are not enough vocals by Debbie Reynolds. MGM SE-4232 ST

CHAPTER 24

South Pacific

But I'm stuck like a dope with this thing called hope
And I can't get it out of my heart

—Oscar Hammerstein II and Richard Rodgers

"Hello?" answered the all-too-familiar voice I had heard on so many Broadway cast records.

"Miss Martin?" I stumbled despite speaking only two words.

"Yes?" she responded in a polite but guarded tone.

"My name is Bruce Hanson, and I was given your number by Harvey Schmidt."

"My goodness," she answered. "How is Harvey?"

"He's just fine. He gave me your number because I am writing a book on the history of *Peter Pan,* and of course I plan to include a chapter on your versions—Broadway and television."

"Well, how nice!" she exclaimed, and I knew that she meant it.

"I was hoping that you would allow me to interview you. Well, not right this minute but at your convenience."

"Of course," she responded with equal enthusiasm. "That would be wonderful! I am here in New York for a benefit performance, but as soon as I get back to California, I would very much love to grant you an interview. I loved being in *Peter Pan*! Let me give the phone to Susan. She'll get your phone number and address and give you mine. Then we can get in touch with you when I get back to California."

The original Broadway cast album for
South Pacific. Columbia ML 4180

The efficient yet warm voice of her assistant and friend Susan Grushkin took over as we traded information. "This is so exciting!" I blurted out. "I never thought I would be able to interview Mary Martin."

"Your project sounds exciting," Grushkin assured me as she jotted down my address and phone number. "We'll get back to you once we have settled in." I wrote down their address as well and hung up the phone feeling as light as a balloon.

About two weeks later my balloon burst when I received a letter from Martin's producer, a Mr. Powers, informing me that his client would not have time to grant me an interview after all. Crushed as I was, common sense immediately took over as I pondered just how to get that interview despite the power of Mr. Powers. The answer did not materialize instantly but rather a few weeks later after I had interviewed Betty Comden and Adolph Green. *I know what I'll do; I'll play Drop that Name. I'll send updates every few weeks on the interviews conducted thus far and merely ask Mary Martin if there is anything that might be missing.*

It took only two letters for Martin to respond. I don't remember much of the content of my letter except that I had interviewed Sondra Lee, who played Tiger Lily, as well as Jule Styne and Comden and Green. But her response was not in a letter but by telephone early one September afternoon. "Hello?" I answered.

"Bruce, this is Mary."

"Mary? Mary Martin?"

"Yes. I have been trying to get ahold of you all summer. Susan and I were in Martha's Vineyard, but we forgot to bring your address or phone number with us. We left it at my home in Rancho Mirage. I tried information, but your phone number is unlisted. Now, I know why mine is unlisted, dear boy, but why is yours?" I explained that someone had been making prank calls to our number so I had decided to take it out of the telephone directory, even paying extra money to do so.

"Tell me how you are doing with the book. I understand that you interviewed Jule [Styne]. Was he difficult?"

"Well, he was a bit grumpy and short of temper," I replied.

"Yes, well. At his age he has a right to be grumpy," she mused. "Who else have you interviewed?" I went down the list of people who at that point included Kathleen Nolan, Mark "Moose" Charlap's widow, singer Sandy Stewart as well as his first wife, Elizabeth Charlap, and a host of other artists involved in various productions of Peter Pan from 1924 through the present. "I even interviewed Charles Eaton, who played John in the Marilyn Miller version of 1924." We chatted awhile about *Peter Pan* and other plays Martin had appeared in.

"We just bought a CD player and had it hooked up to our stereo," Martin went on. "We listened to *The Sound of Music* and could not get over how clear it sounds. It's as if we recorded it yesterday!"

"Yes, it sounds fantastic," I agreed. "Do you have *Jennie, South Pacific,* and *Peter Pan*? Because they sound great on CD too." Our conversation went on for a few more minutes, and then Martin asked me to write my questions and send them to her so she could answer them thoughtfully in a letter typed by Susan. I wanted to yell, "Please don't type them! I want them in your handwriting!" But that would have sounded too much like a fan, and I was trying to sound as professional as possible. A few weeks later I received the typed letter and inserted the information in my book. About this time I heard again from Harvey Schmidt, inquiring how my interview had gone.

"You know she's dying, don't you?"

"Who's dying?"

"Mary," he said quietly. "They discovered cancer. That's why she had to back out of our musical, *Grover's Corner*." Martin had appeared in *I Do, I Do,* a musical that Harvey wrote with Tom Jones. He went on to say that her illness was probably the reason Mr. Powers had vetoed the original interview—that he was worried it would be too taxing, with all her other commitments.

"I am so lucky that she took the time to call me back and grant me the interview," I said. "I was worried that I wouldn't hear from her because I was not professional sounding."

"Bruce, it's probably because you did not sound professional that Mary agreed to let you interview her," Harvey mused.

About three years later, after Mary Martin passed away and my book was published, I received a couple of letters from her daughter, Heller Halliday DeMeritt, informing me that she loved my book and that her mother had taken an instant liking to me. I couldn't get over it. Mary Martin had discussed me. Mary Martin liked me.

In a review of her performance as character Nellie Forbush in *South Pacific*, Kenneth Tynan said that she reminded him of something that Aldous Huxley had written about the minor Caroline poets: "They spoke in their natural voices and it was poetry." He added, "While Ethel Merman was an entire brass section and Carol Channing was a parade, Miss Martin remained natural and exactingly true to life—and it was poetry."

CHAPTER 25

The Voices of Patti Page

How much is that doggie in the window?
The one with the waggly tail.

—Bob Merrill and Ingrid Reuterskiöld, 1952

On February 1, 2009, my dog Blue died. The next day I wrote an e-mail to my friends and colleagues describing just what he meant to me and then forgot about it until years later when I decided I wanted to include it in this book of essays. Unfortunately, I had erased the e-mail as well as the many sympathetic responses I had received that same day. Thinking that no one would possibly have saved it, I decided to write to my colleagues and friends anyway, hoping that at least one person might not have erased it. To my amazement, three people wrote back within an hour saying that they had kept the e-mail because they were touched by the content. Here it is:

Am I Blue?

Even as I write this, a *thankfully* small cynical voice from within is nagging me with "He was just a dog. Many people have dogs that are cute, loyal, and loving. What made Blue so special?"

Blue, along with another Dalmatian, Mona, was a gift for my son about fifteen years ago when our first dog, a Siberian Husky named Snow, was stolen. Drew was devastated and insisted that we place signs all over the Ghent area of Norfolk in hopes that someone might have seen her. A few months later he asked if we could get another dog, but this time perhaps we could also find a friend for that dog. In other words, Drew wanted two dogs. And not just any dogs; he wanted Dalmatians! At the time, I had no idea what I was in for, as my only knowledge of the breed was from Walt Disney and a few vintage photographs from assorted fire houses. However, like many parents, I gave in in spite of my ignorance. We purchased six-week-old Mona from a breeder in Virginia Beach, and a few hours later, five-week-old Blue joined us from Norfolk. Blue was extremely small and timid with too many black spots and a large black spot surrounding one eye. Despite my arguments for a livelier puppy, Drew was set on Blue. In fact, I had to pay more for him, as he had one blue eye.

The Voices of Patti Page featuring "How Much is That Doggie in the Window?" Mercury MG-20100

Even before I had finished filling out the check, Drew had suggested that we name our new puppy Spot "because he has so many spots." I suggested that we wait a bit to see what their personalities were like before we named the new additions to our family. Secretly, I was hoping to name the dogs after some great literary characters, but that wish was lost even before we arrived home. With Drew's eyes glued to the backseat of the car, Blue slept peacefully alongside his moaning counterpart. Drew quickly named her Mona. "Mona Lisa," I added with some satisfaction.

"And this, this is Blue Boy, he added, naming him after the Gainsborough painting. I looked at my son, and my heart swelled with love for him as he carefully pet his new puppies—Mona and Blue. However, within a few hours it became obvious that Blue Boy would simply be called Blue and that Blue was deaf. Yes, he could hear if you shouted at the top of your lungs, but otherwise he just looked at you with puzzlement. Of course there was no bringing him back despite the warranty, as Drew was already in love with him. "Who would love him now?" he asked me when I suggested the absurdity of returning him. Funny, isn't it, wanting a warranty on life?

The veterinarian we selected had raised Dalmatians as a child, so he was quite helpful with hints in training Blue. "Never surprise him from behind," he said in a most serious tone to Drew, "and he will always be loving and sweet. And try developing a sign language to train him." Thus, if you spotted the four of us on a corner in Ghent, a section of Norfolk, Virginia, you might have seen the most ridiculous yet endearing sight as we taught both dogs to "stop," "sit," or "go seep" (our version of "go to sleep") with our own animated version of sign language. Blue was most fun to watch as he jumped like a gazelle up and down through the Colley

Avenue monkey grass while Mona remained on the sidewalk with her truck driver stride.

At home it was another story; Dalmatians can be a needy crew and our dogs were no exception. While Blue had the gentlest disposition, Mona was selfish, mean, and domineering. I didn't like her, nor, for that matter, did I care much for Blue. They were my son's dogs; I was merely their caretaker. As they grew, so did their appetite for destruction. And what began with a few books and record albums grew to monumental proportions with them eating the walls, floor, and cabinets in the kitchen of my new (old) house. I was constantly threatening to "get rid of them" until one day it became obvious that Mona was pregnant. And that is when I fell in love with my son's dogs.

It was a late August morning when Mona went into labor. I woke up at 8:00 to find her shaking and weeping next to a small white puppy still in its embryonic sac. He was dead; stillborn. But even as Mona cried, she was in the midst of birthing another so I gently opened the sac to help. *Oh my God, what do I do next? Spank the puppy?* Fortunately, common sense prevailed and I instinctively stroked the puppy until she started breathing on her own. Mona was quick to catch on, and she was nibbling at the sac while simultaneously cleaning her baby with her tongue. Forty-five minutes later, as the next arrival was working his way out, Mona had become a pro. She was amazingly gentle as she worked at the sacs and puppies even before they were completely in this new world. And all the while, Blue watched from a safe distance. Mona had made it quite clear to her mate that he was not allowed to be near her litter. It was almost midnight when she finally delivered her last puppy; there were fifteen in all. Five did not make it, and Mona cried for each of her lost offspring while Blue watched the whole proceedings with his head resting on his paws. He never left her side except to be taken outside.

Poor Ol' Blue was so unhappy when Mona would not allow him near their puppies.

For the next few days it was wondrous to watch Mona, who until this new adventure, had lived up to the name "bitch." She was the most beautiful "mommy." Blue often looked sad during this brief period, confused that Mona would not allow him to be near her or their puppies and perhaps because Mona and her brood were receiving so much attention. Then, one day, about a week later, I came home for lunch with Kathy, a friend of mine, to show off the new "first family." We quietly entered the house so as not to wake Mona in case she was sleeping. Indeed, she was asleep, with five of her puppies nuzzled close for warmth. Where were the other five? There, on the other side of the kitchen was Blue with his puppies where he was ever so gently cleaning them. I watched quietly in awe. There was neither time to get a camera nor time to videotape the event. Instead, all I could do was smile as my eyes filled with tears. For at that moment, at that very moment, I knew I loved my dogs. I loved Mona despite her disposition (which would return a few months later). And I loved Blue. I loved Blue for his extraordinary love, his loyalty, and his patience with Mona, their litter, Drew, and me.

Ol' Blue died last night. He had not been doing so well the last few weeks, but he was cognizant and in no pain. Dale lovingly took care of him while I was at school and while I stayed in Norfolk on weeknights. He would walk "the old man" and gently help him negotiate the steps of our house in Petersburg. This morning I buried Ol' Blue in our garden, where he constantly wandered in attempts to slurp water out of the birdbath. I don't believe in God, Heaven, or any sort of afterlife. I wish I did. Yet Ol' Blue and other creatures like him most certainly have a special place even after they no longer walk this earth, after they christen our bushes and trees, eat our favorite books and records, or just run to the door with wagging tails and tongues sloppily drooling simply because we came home. Memories: they are our final legacy from those we love. Blue now shares that space with others I have loved and lost. And I share this memory with you, my family away from my family.

CHAPTER 26

Christmastime

Don we now our gay apparel
Fa-la-la, la-la-la, la-la-la.
Troll the ancient Yule time carol,
Fa la la la la, la la la la

—TRADITIONAL WELSH CAROL WITH LYRICS BY THOMAS OLIPHANT

LIKE MANY PEOPLE, I COUNT Christmas as my favorite holiday. Not only does it relate to Christians with its enchanting story of the birth of Jesus, but it also stimulates the most positive feelings in a secular fashion. It is the season of giving, showing kindness and goodwill to others, singing Christmas carols, and decorating our house with lights and a Christmas tree. Every season since I could hold money in my wallet, I looked forward to perusing the record bins of my favorite department stores for new Christmas albums. Even today I still check with Amazon.com and other online sources for new albums or compilations of older material.

Equally special to me is decorating our home. Dale is very strict on certain elements of decorating: fresh holly, berries, real garland, and, of course, a freshly cut Christmas tree—tradition! Drew, who is now married, has always spent Christmas with his mother, but since 2009 we have hosted Christmas Day with our friend Beth and her sons Josh, Adam, and Eli. They have become for us, and we for them, a second family. Usually Adam, a former student of mine, will arrive a few days earlier than his siblings to help decorate the tree and wrap presents. On Christmas Day the boys drive up from Norfolk with their mother (unless Josh is overseas, where he is stationed in the armed forces) and we play Christmas music, eat hors d'oeuvres, open presents, and then go for a twenty-minute walk looking at the lights of private residences of historic Petersburg while Dale adds the finishing touches to the holiday meal. We come back to a candlelit chandelier shimmering above a beautiful golden brown turkey stuffed with oranges, dressing, and parsley. A few times we have even been lucky enough to return lightly dusted with the gift of a white Christmas.

Christmastime was released in 1946 on four 78 rpm records and reissued as a 45 rpm record set in 1950. Kenny Baker, Deanna Durbin, and Judy Garland perform. Judy's "The Star of the East" and "The Birthday of a King" were recorded in 1941. Decca 9-73

Before we moved to Petersburg, Dale and I lived ten miles apart in North Carolina. His house, in Murfreesboro, was a beautiful, historic Greek revival home built in 1830, and mine was a lovely 1870 Victorian cottage on Main Street in Woodland. Woodland is a small town with a population of perhaps eight hundred. During the first Christmas season in my new house, my parents sent a huge box of Christmas decorations that I had grown up with. "Your brothers don't want them," my mother had written in a note, "so they're yours." I was thrilled! Inside were strings of lights with big colorful bulbs, glass ornaments that went back to the forties, and two large lanterns depicting Santa Claus and Christmas trees on the white transparent panels. I immediately began decorating.

Meanwhile, Dale was preparing his house as part of a Christmas tour for Murfreesboro. With the theme "Christmas Memories," Dale accented his tree with small family photographs. Because he was in charge of the entire tour, he didn't get to work on his tree until the afternoon of that evening's first tour. Dale would not allow any help even as he dashed to the local CVS Pharmacy to make copies of his photos and insert them in small, festive holiday frames. He did ask me if I could be the docent in his house. I agreed: a chance to be onstage! Meanwhile, I was happily hanging my kitschy ornaments and lights on my Victorian house.

That night Dale's house looked festive: apples, oranges, and a pineapple adorned his front door, and there were fresh garlands and candles inside. *Why the pineapple?* He told me it symbolized being welcome to a home during colonial times. The tree was magnificent with its photos and white and blue lights. Throughout the tours I emphasized how important family was to Dale— true—as well as his tradition of decorating his trees with photos—*untrue,* although to be fair, we have used photos every year since. As I was speaking to the tourists about the tree, I noticed that among Dale's family portraits and snapshots was a picture of my best friend from Norfolk, Michelle, who was going to be spending Christmas Day with us. Without a pause in my monologue, I further noticed that many of the photos were of men and boys: men Dale had had relationships with at one time or another before he met me and boys he had had crushes on in high school. But my picture was nowhere to be found! "There was no time to get a photo of you," he blurted quickly and quietly when he stopped by to check up on me.

"But Michelle is my best friend, and that photo you have of her was taken at my house last year during Christmas!"

"Yes, that's because I love you," he answered slyly. "And I love your friends." The next night I placed my photo on his tree.

A day later I was eating lunch with my friends Margaret and Anna, when Anna told me that the owner of the supermarket on Main Street had asked her if she was sure I was gay.

"Of course he's gay," she assured him.

"Well, I'm not sure," he retorted. "Aren't gay men supposed to have good taste? His house has the ugliest decorations I've ever seen!" When she told me this, I was crushed. Here I thought my house looked so cool and a straight man was saying it was ugly. When I told Dale, he merely laughed and told me to forget about it. But Dale did not.

The following Christmas Dale asked me if I wanted help decorating my house. I replied that I was going to do only the inside. "Nonsense," he said and produced an ax from his car. He walked to the wooded area next my house, began chopping down pine trees and holly branches, and tacked them around my door and windows. Then he pulled out strings of small white lights from the trunk of his car and intertwined them with his fresh garland. Finally, he went into my kitchen and constructed the most tasteful and elegant arrangement of lemons, apples, and pineapple I have ever seen.

"Why are you doing all this" I finally asked.

"Ain't nobody gonna say my boyfriend ain't gay!"

CHAPTER 27

Fiddler on the Roof

I don't remember growing older
When did they?

—SHELDON HARNICK AND JERRY BOCK

ONE OF MY FAVORITE MUSICALS is probably on most people's best-show list, *Fiddler on the Roof.* I'm listening to the Mono version of this musical right now as I write this difficult chapter. You see, my mother is dying of cancer in California where she has lived with my stepfather, Allen, for about the last fifteen years. They moved to a beautiful retirement village near Laguna Beach, where they decided to live instead of Florida, where most of my other relatives eventually retired. The weather, the beaches, the pools, and the various clubs they belong to: these assets have practically made it a paradise. For me, the positive aspect of their relocation to the West Coast is that they have lived so far away. And the negative aspect is that they have lived so far away.

I don't think my parents ever understood me, nor, I'm afraid, did I understand them.

About twenty-five years ago, Allen, asked me what I taught. I was quite disappointed, because I had been teaching art and theater for eight years. Yet a year or so later, they came to visit me after my divorce and attended a rehearsal for a play I was in, *Angels in America*. There, in the audience of the theater, Mom knitted and Allen read the sports section of the newspaper while my character, Prior Walter, who was dying of AIDS, ran around the stage blaspheming a holy book, which was sure to shock them. They knew that the year before, I had appeared nude onstage in the first part of the play. As I walked across the stage to meet with an angel, my director asked me to drop my robe so that I would appear in my pajamas. I looked out to where my parents were sitting; Allen gazed up from his newspaper while Mom looked over her glasses. I gave some sort of gesture to comfort them, to let them know I was not going to be nude in this play. I felt sure they were revolted by the whole rehearsal. But instead, they took me to dinner at a local restaurant where Allen told me that he had never realized how much work went into a play. "I'm proud of you," he said simply.

And then, a few years ago, out of the blue, my mother called to let me know again how proud they were of me. "You were the dreamer," she explained. "We never thought you'd amount to anything."

"Um, thanks, Mom—I think."

"What I'm trying to say is that we expected that we would be helping you financially most of your adult life." I guess I had stopped trying to please them when I married for the first time at the age of twenty-three. They thought my older brother should wed first.

Listening to *Fiddler on the Roof,* I am browsing through the liner notes and find myself aching with a deep longing for something from the past. Most of the singers on the album are deceased now: Zero Mostel, Maria Karnilova, Bert Convey, Beatrice Arthur, and Leonard Frey. Some died of natural causes, and others were victims of the gay epidemic of the eighties. But in 1964, they were a constant for a ten-year-old stuck on musical comedy. They were my friends. And although my parents always fought loudly and sometimes I found their arguments frightening, they were my friends too. I just didn't know it at the time.

The original cast album of *Fiddler on the Roof.* RCA LSO-1093.
My parents saw the show shortly after it opened in 1964 and
immediately bought the record for me. In my junior high
school music class, we were allowed to perform any song once
a week, but the songs from *Fiddler* were the most popular. We
often sang the title song; however, it was not even in the play.
"Fiddler on the Roof" was created specifically for sheet music
sales with lyrics written by Sheldon Harnick who adapted some
of the themes from "Tradition" by Jerry Bock. It read in part:

A way upon my roof I see the strangest sight,
A fiddler on the roof who's up there day and night.

CHAPTER 28

Cinderella

Impossible things are happening every day.

—Oscar Hammerstein II and Richard Rodgers

For eight years I taught at a middle school in New Jersey with only a small amount of involvement in theater. The vice principal, who was there for many years, owned a small theatrical company, and each year he would stage an elaborate musical revue using the talents (or lack of) of every eighth grader. Casting was based on the costumes he had at hand and who could fit in them. And at least one number in each review required most of the boys to appear shirtless. The first time I witnessed this Ziegfeld extravaganza, I think the boys were all dressed in diapers. *Shades of Joshua Logan!* I thought to myself. Yet, despite the campy and overtly homosexual overtones, the parents never caught on, and this annual fest of pubescent flesh was a highly anticipated attraction in the show.

Then, almost out of the blue, the vice principal either was either fired or resigned or whatever else can happen to someone of his stature in the community who is suspected of child molestation. Ironically, it was during an investigation of a teacher charged with the same behavior that the vice principal's name came up. When asked if the teacher had ever behaved inappropriately with them, the young male students, all of whom had appeared in the diaper number, exclaimed, "No, never! But the one you should be investigating is the

vice principal!" Ironically, the teacher, despite being acquitted of child molestation, had to quit teaching and never lived down the accusations. The vice
principal, on the other hand, quietly disappeared without a trial or any publicity. Such were (and are) the mechanisms of many school districts: protect the
administrators at all costs and throw the teachers to the lions.

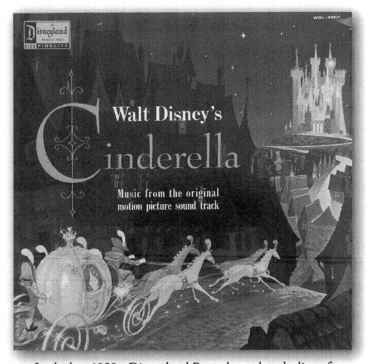

In the late 1950s, Disneyland Records produced a line of
albums marketed toward adults. They included stunning
album covers, extensive (for that period) background music,
and the familiar vocals. These rare soundtracks became
known as the WDL series. Along with *Cinderella*, there
was *Snow White, Sleeping Beauty, Dumbo, Bambi, Alice in
Wonderland*, and *Pinocchio*. Disneyland WDL 4007 The
Walt Disney Company. © Disney Enterprises, Inc.

By now you must be asking yourself, *What does this have to do with*
Cinderella? You see, for several years I had hoped that I might direct plays
that were more appropriate for the middle-school-aged children of this school

where I taught art for eight years. With the loss of the principal and vice principal I was finally allowed to do so. The first production was a forgettable thing called *Tumbleweeds*, followed by *Peter Pan*, and then Rodgers and Hammerstein's *Cinderella*.

For the scenery, our choral music teacher suggested that we incorporate a revolving set with the throne room on one side and Cinderella's shabby fireplace on the other. The only problem was that the set weighed over five hundred pounds! There was no way my small crew of dedicated twelve year-olds was going to be able to turn it without help. Breaking my rule of letting my students run the show, I was backstage with them, pulling the revolving set. On closing night during intermission, while turning this revolving nightmare once too many times, my kids suddenly stopped and looked at me in silence.

"What's wrong?" I asked, looking down to see if my zipper was open or something dreadful like that. No one would answer. "What's wrong? What did I do?"

"It's not what you did," a brave one finally answered. "It's what you said."

"All right, what did I say?" No answer. "Oh c'mon, what did I say?"

"You said—you said, 'I hate this fucking set!'"

"What? You're kidding! There's no way I could have said such a thing!" I protested. "Impossible!"

"But you still said it, Mr. Hanson."

"Really? You're not fooling me?"

"No!" all of the crew answered in unison. "You said, 'I hate this fucking set!'"

"And you know what?" asked the brave one. "We hate this fucking set too!" We all laughed until we realized that we were getting too loud backstage and it was close to starting act 2.

"Places!"

CHAPTER 29

Till the Clouds Roll By

As I wash my dishes, I'll be following a plan
Till I see the brightness in every pot and pan

—Jerome Kern and Buddy G. DeSylva

Although *The Wizard of Oz*, *Kiss Me Kate*, and *The Unsinkable Molly Brown* were the first soundtrack records I bought after selling off my comic book collection, it was *Till the Clouds Roll By* that opened my eyes to the MGM sound. Many years later composer Harvey Schmidt, composer of *The Fantasticks* and *I Do, I Do*, became a friend while I was doing research on *Peter Pan*. At dinner one night he said that our musical theater training was through the University of MGM. Thank goodness for the many used-record and used-book shops throughout New York City that I frequented as a child, for it was through those venues that I was first exposed to "out-of-print" soundtracks.

It was in a little secondhand book and record shop just off Cooper Square in New York City run by a sweet middle-aged couple where I bought my first used record album. The store was amid several head shops specializing in drug paraphernalia, incense burners, Peter Max posters, and glow-in-the-dark art. It was 1967, the dawn of nostalgia. The walls of the shop also had huge posters, but these were blowups of photos of the husband-and-wife proprietors from the 1940s. I remember thinking that the wife looked like Laverne Andrews of the Andrews Sisters.

Till the Clouds Roll By is the 1946 MGM musical that set
the tradition for soundtrack albums to follow. This 45
rpm record set that was released in 1950 is more difficult
to find than the 1947 78 rpm album. MGM K-1

As I browsed through the records, I noticed a title that I was familiar
with, *Singin' in the Rain*, but when I turned the album over to read the liner
notes, I realized that there was another soundtrack as well and that the *Singin'
in the Rain* photo was actually the back cover. The front of the album featured
a color photograph of a circus scene with—I recognized her immediately from
The Wizard of Oz—Judy Garland. Inside the gatefold album were more photos with more stars I recognized from my first soundtrack records: Debbie
Reynolds and Kathryn Grayson. June Allyson I had just seen on television
in *Her Highness and the Bellboy*, and some of the songs listed from *Clouds* included excerpts from *Showboat*. The vinyl was in great condition and housed
in an inside paper sleeve that advertised other MGM musicals, including *In
the Good Old Summertime* back-to-back with *An American in Paris*.

"How much is this record, please?" I asked, expecting it to be more than five dollars.

"For you, one dollar!" the husband answered.

"Wow, that is amazing!

"It's not that amazing," his wife said. "All of our records are one dollar."

"Well, I will be coming back to your shop again," I promised as I paid the dollar plus tax. "I still have enough money left over to buy an Orange Julius with an egg." That night I listened to the record over and over again and slept with it by my pillow. I was hooked.

Over the years I bought the various editions of *Till the Clouds Roll By* even though I never saw the film. The 78 rpm album was released in 1947, which was not only MGM's first-ever commercially released album, but also established a record genre—the soundtrack album. Four years later a ten-inch LP was issued, and then it was coupled with *Gentlemen Prefer Blondes* in a truncated edition in 1953. There was also a four record 45 rpm album, a two-record edition of 45 EPs, and the Metro version in the mid-sixties. In the early 1970s I bought an imported version from England in the Village and then ran to the 13th Street Repertory Theatre for a rehearsal. "What have you got there, Brucie?" asked Bill Solly, the resident songwriter who later wrote the enchanting and sophisticated musical comedy *Boy Meets Boy*.

"They've released the MGM musicals in England!" I practically shouted. "And they're selling them at Doubleday!" Bill opened the gatefold jacket.

"Did you happen to notice who wrote the liner notes?" he asked with a devilish grin. He handed it back to me, and there was his name.

"This makes it perfect!" I answered. Actually, even better was that on the same day, Bill informed me that one of the actors was dropping out of *100 Hundred Miles from Nowhere* and that I, as understudy, would be replacing him. It was a perfect day!

Move forward to May 11, 2008, to what I can only describe as a cloak-and-dagger scene: I was bidding furiously against another eBay member for several MGM Studios twelve-inch playback discs from *Till the Clouds Roll By*, a highly fictionalized account of the life and career of Jerome Kern. Playback discs are the records that were used on the set for the musical performers to sing with during filming. During the making of *The Broadway Melody*, MGM's first "all talking, all singing, all dancing" musical of 1929, the musical numbers were shot "live" with the orchestra out of camera range. During the editing, Irving Thalberg was dissatisfied with a Technicolor musical number, "The Wedding of the Painted Doll," and decided to have it reshot. Douglas Shearer, the recording director, suggested that they use the existing soundtrack, which was perfectly fine, as a playback for re-filming of the number. This innovative idea not only saved the studio the extra money to pay the musicians again but also became a standard practice for Hollywood musicals to get the best musical sound. Because the singing had to match the dialogue of the films, no reverb (echo) was added, resulting in a more natural sounding recording. Interestingly, when MGM records first rereleased their soundtracks on twelve-inch LPs in 1960, they added too much reverb. However, the same albums were remastered when the record company changed their record label from yellow and black to a more contemporary look and they reverted to the original flat recordings, which I generally prefer. The lyrics for the songs written for *The Broadway Melody* were by Arthur Freed, who later became MGM's (if not the world's) best producer of musical films. His films include *Singin' in the Rain*, *Showboat*, *An American in Paris*, *Meet Me in St. Louis*, *Gigi*, *On the Town*, and *Till the Clouds Roll By*, and he nurtured the careers of Judy Garland, Gene Kelly, June Allyson, Cyd Charise, and later added Fred Astaire to the roster of his repertory company.

I did not the win Frank Sinatra's cover of "Old Man River" or Judy Garland's "Who," complete with Kay Thompson's added verse to the Kern-Hammerstein II song, which sold for several hundred dollars apiece. However, I was thrilled with the nine discs I was able to purchase, which included Judy singing "Look for the Silver Lining," June Allyson's "Cleopatterer" and "Leave It to Jane," Kathryn Grayson and her then hubby, Johnny Johnston, performing "I've Told Every Little Star," and key background music.

A day or two after paying for the records I received an e-mail from the person who had been bidding against me. At that time eBay not only allowed its bidders and sellers to openly see the competition but provided e-mail addresses for contact. He wrote that he was sorry for bidding up the price I paid for my discs, that he wanted high-quality dubs (another name for playbacks) to supply the cues (orchestral, instrumental, or choral parts which are timed to begin and end at a specific point during the film in order to enhance the drama) that were not held in the archives of the MGM recordings to the library, and asked if it would be possible to obtain dubs. I had no idea what library he was referring to. He added that he was not bidding on the next several coming up for auction, but if I won the playback records, would he be able to borrow them to record? In return he could send me something rare from his huge soundtrack collection. He signed his e-mail Terrence.

I responded that if I did win, which I did, I would indeed make dubs for him.

We exchanged a few e-mails, and I agreed to send a CD of the recordings, because I had just purchased a new 78 rpm stylus for my Dual turntable. However, Terrence reminded me that the records I held were actually recorded at 80 rpm and not 78 rpm. He added that he owned a turntable on which they could properly be played and recorded for producer George Feltenstein, who was looking for all of the pre-recordings from the film to ideally one day produce a soundtrack album for Rhino records. I wanted to share the sound of the records, but Dale reminded me how much I had paid for them and that this was a stranger asking me to send them to him.

On June 22, I wrote an e-mail to film maker Peter Fitzgerald of FitzFilms, a friend of Feltenstein's. Together they had coproduced *That's Entertainment, Part III*:

Dear Peter Fitzgerald:

A few years ago I wrote to you complimenting you on your documentary films that you have created for the Warner Bros. DVD releases of MGM films. You were kind enough to write back. A few weeks ago I won (on eBay) several 80 rpm acetate records from the soundtrack of *Till the Clouds Roll By*. These are 12" records with white labels bearing the MGM logo in blue print...I received an email from the other bidder who wrote that he was a friend of George Feltenstein's and was always on the lookout for these rare records for Feltenstein's Rhino Records releases. In particular, they were looking for all of the studio recordings from *Till the Clouds Roll By* to create a CD…I wrote back saying I would certainly share the soundtracks…there were several discs that sold for over three hundred dollars apiece but I did manage to win eight [sic] discs.

As a writer I have been burned when original materials were not returned to me. I am asking if you could please pass this email along to George Feltenstein to see if he is indeed interested in these records. I would gladly lend them to him and/or his friend "Terrence" but I just want to know that this is all legit. Some of the records sound wonderful and others not as good, as it appears that the plastic inserts they were mailed in left a heavy residue of plastic. The records were delivered the week of that terrible heat wave and were actually hot when I unwrapped them…

Thank you,
Bruce

Peter answered immediately, saying that he was a big fan of *Till the Clouds Roll By* and would pass my e-mail along.

I wrote to Terrence saying that I would at least make a recording of the records for him. Then I received another e-mail from him apologizing for the lapse in time between e-mails. Again he offered to send me dubs of rare recordings from film soundtracks. He elaborated on the possibility of George Feltenstein producing an official release of *Clouds* if he could obtain enough material. Naturally, I wanted to do whatever I could to help make this a reality. I heard from Terrence again later that summer when he said that George Feltenstein had told him that I had contacted Peter Fitzgerald but that he understood my reservations as I did not know him. He went on:

"I'd welcome the chance to speak to you by phone and tell you some things that I'm not comfortable writing that I think might ease your comfort level.

There's nothing mysterious here, and it will make perfect sense if and when we speak. Like you, I take precautions with things. Let me know if you desire to do so." Terrence offered to clean the records and play them on a record player with the proper speed and stylus. In particular, he was interested in the scoring cues used in the film when the fictitious character played by Van Heflin was on his deathbed. Most of the recording, which features singer Loulie Jean Norman, were in the MGM archive in two channels, but he wrote that my recording could be used to append the ending. It was apparent that Terrence was extremely excited about the scoring cues for *Clouds*.

I wrote back:

Dear Terrence,

Thanks so much for your understanding email. When my book, *The Peter Pan Chronicles,* was published, an editor at the publishing house took off with a few key items. This happened again when a film company "borrowed" some rare books of mine for their research and never returned them. When I won these MGM acetates I received emails from several people with requests to borrow them to record. I guess you can see why I was taking precautions...
Yes, I'd love to chat with you on the phone. Please let me know your number. But again, thank you for not being cross with me at checking up on you. I felt terrible doing so.

Sincerely,
Bruce

By this time, I was quite curious about Terrence. Who in the business named Terrence would care this much about film and sound preservation and have such contacts? I decided it must be playwright Terrence McNally, who loves musicals and whose play *Love! Valour! Compassion!* I had appeared in in Richmond just a few years before. How's that for an assumption?

On July 13, Terrence wrote again asking when he could call, since he would be in New York for a few days. In those days I hardly ever kept my phone on. Actually, my students tell me I still do that. Naturally, Terrence was unable to get hold of me. He wrote again on July 31:

> Bruce,
>
> Hello. I'll try and call you in the next day or so and if I can't reach you I'll send another email removing the veil of mystery.
>
> T.

I wrote back:

> I am at a writing workshop tonight until 9:00 so my phone will be turned off till then.
>
> Bruce

And then the surprise!

> Bruce,
>
> ...My name is Michael Feinstein and I'm not a Terrence at all, so your musings as to which Terrence it might have been were in vain... Your willingness to share what you acquired on eBay is very kind and it is rare these days...So that's the story in a nut shell and I apologize for stringing you along! I'll look forward to continuing our dialogue about this world of music and theatre.
>
> Sincerely,
> Michael

Michael Feinstein! Wow! Of course I had heard of him. I was thrilled. Not only was "Terrence" legit but he was also Michael Feinstein: the talented interpreter of the *Great American Songbook* and an archivist of rare recordings who aids many in the record industry in reintroducing great recordings on CD.

I tried to calm down so my e-mail would not sound so much like that of a fan. I sent the records to Michael, and in return he sent some wonderful recordings by Rosemary Clooney, minus the studio reverb, as well as some other rare and fun stuff. A month or so later I received my records, which were much cleaner than when I sent them, along with a CD of the songs recorded at the proper speed. He was genuinely grateful and gracious. I wrote a note of thanks and included the following:

> I've been working on a group of essays for a book, tentatively titled *For the Record: Confessions of a Vinyl Addict*. They are writings about my collecting records and how they have influenced my life, mostly in a humorous vein. There is one about Rosemary Clooney/*White Christmas* and another on MGM soundtracks that might amuse you.
>   Hope your trip to NYC was fruitful and fun. Thanks again!
>
> Sincerely,
> Bruce

Shortly afterward, I signed a contract to update and revise my book *The Peter Pan Chronicles*. Thus it was almost four years until I returned to writing *For the Record*. As for Michael Feinstein, he continued with his recordings and nightclub appearances and married his longtime partner, Terrence Flannery. *Terrence! Of course!* I sent them a ceramic casserole I threw on the wheel as a wedding present and received a very sweet thank-you note. Michael also has written a wonderful book, *The Gershwins and Me*. I have never met him in person or even chatted with him since, but I am very grateful for what he has done to preserve recordings of the *Great American Songbook*. And who knows, I might even meet Michael someday. I can wait…at least till the clouds roll by. Or is it "till the cows come home?"

CHAPTER 30

High Society

Well did you evah?
What a swell party this is.

—COLE PORTER

I HAVE NEVER BEEN PARTICULARLY good at throwing a party. My first was in high school: a Halloween party during which all my guests left as early as possible as they lied, telling me what a great time they had had. Early in college, before I moved out of my parents' home, I threw a small, intimate party for twenty-five while they were in Europe. Unfortunately, over two hundred people showed up with liquor, beer, pot, and cigarettes, with couples and triples sleeping in every bed of my parents' house. Somehow, during all of the madness, the only damage was in the basement rec room, when, during a wild jitterbug re-creation, I lifted my dancing partner so high, her feet went through the ceiling. Luckily, because the tile was in a hidden corner of the room, it was not clearly visible and thus remained hidden for twelve years. It was during a visit with my year-old son, Drew, that I surprised my mother, who was cleaning downstairs.

"Mom?" I called out from the top of the landing.

"Oh my God!" she exclaimed. "You scared the life out of me! And look what I've done!" Her broom handle had poked right through the hole in the ceiling that I had created years before.

"Mom, you didn't do that. Remember that party I had when you were in Europe? The one your neighbors told you about? Well..." We both laughed.

The MGM soundtrack of *High Society* on Capitol Records features a first rate score by Cole Porter and an outstanding cast including Bing Crosby, Frank Sinatra, Louis Armstrong, Grace Kelly, and Celeste Holm. But look for the mono version rather than the stereo. Capitol W750

Move ahead twenty-five years: One of my coworkers at my school, Callie, was pregnant, and I thought it would be a nice gesture for my department to throw her a surprise shower. Everyone agreed. In planning the refreshments, I volunteered to bring a cake and soft drinks, including pineapple soda, while others shared the responsibility for paper cups, napkins, plates, and forks. One art teacher—I'll call her Darlene—told me that she had asked the others what they wanted to eat and drink and that they had said they did not want soda or cake but wanted hummus instead. Therefore, that was what she was going to bring. Okay, that was fine with me, but I was still going to buy cake and sodas. I asked each person to bring a small gift.

Two weeks later we surprised Callie in a small room off the school library. A table was set with a cute paper tablecloth, matching napkins and paper plates, and a cake decorated with lacy sugar flowers. On the side were three bottles of soda: Coke, Sprite, and pineapple. Oh, yes, and a small container of hummus. No crackers, no chips to dip with, nothing!

The music teachers arrived a few minutes late (so what else was new?) but without any refreshments, and worse, without presents for Callie. Even as the others tried to hide their shock over their empty-handed colleagues, everyone chomped down the cake and finished the sodas.

Oh, I almost forgot: the pineapple soda was the first soda consumed, and the hummus just sat there. Well did you evah? What a swell party it was.

CHAPTER 31

Good-Bye Yellow
Brick Road

*When all the world is a hopeless jumble and the raindrops tumble all around
Heaven opens its magic lane*

— E.Y. "Yip" Harburg and Harold Arlen

I KNOW WHAT YOU'RE THINKING: "Good-Bye Yellow Brick Road" is by Elton John. And I must confess that I toyed with the idea of using "Candle in the Wind" as the epigraph for this final entry. In fact, I bought the newly remastered vinyl of this classic rock album just a few days before I began writing this chapter. But as much as I love that song, indeed, the whole album, it reminds me too much of the tragedies of Marilyn Monroe and Princess Diana. Therefore, I have chosen an epigraph from a seemingly more innocent period because this last chapter is about an innocent. And it did not seem appropriate to add an image here. The present-day, for all of its technology and communication literally at our finger tips while violence habitually prevails, is often difficult for me to understand.

This much I can comprehend: one of my favorite students, Latisha, died a week ago today. I was certainly prepared for this tragedy. Latisha primed not just me but all of her friends and teachers for the inevitable. I have changed her name for this book to protect her family's privacy.

About two months before her death, Latisha, a homebound learner, asked our administrators if she could say good-bye to all of us in one room. She knew that the radiation treatments she had been receiving on and off for the last year and a half had failed to stop the growth of cancer behind her eye. She knew that almost half of her face was now missing; she knew that she had already lost one eye and the second had decreased in vision; she knew that she was working against time to graduate high school; and she knew that in the next few weeks her health would deteriorate with an alarming speed. In short, Latisha knew that she was dying.

To understand this remarkable young girl, you must know that by no means was she a role model before her illness. As a tenth grader Latisha signed up for my acting class and immediately established herself as a chatterbox and a genuine pain in the ass. Our first six months together were a constant struggle for me to maintain some sort of sanity while attempting to teach Latisha to respect her peers by watching them without interrupting and talking to them during their scenes. This was not an easy task. One day, I had finally had enough.

Going to the back of the auditorium, I told an angry Latisha that she would have to sit away from the class until she could learn some theater etiquette. Folding her arms in defiance, she quietly but clearly muttered, "So that's the way it is, Mr. Hanson?"

"That's the way it is," I snapped back, folding my arms in the same manner.

"Fine," she answered, and sat down with the biggest frown imaginable. The next hour was unbearable for us both: for Latisha because she desperately wanted to get on that stage and act, and for me because I recognized her love of performing.

At the beginning of our next class, Latisha apologized for her disruptive behavior and gave me her word that she would improve. Although I accepted her apology graciously, I did not completely believe that she could live up to her promise. Boy, was I wrong! Not only did she commit herself to changing her old ways, but she progressed as a performer onstage. Within the next few weeks she was in every scene she could possibly handle, so that by the end of the semester, she found herself part of a small group made up of actors from all of my classes who would perform in *Fractured Fairy Tales* for elementary school children. Although not a big deal in the larger scheme of things, to my classes this was considered an honor awarded based on their talent, professionalism, perseverance, and ability to get along with their fellow thespians. Their work had to be entertaining and funny for inner-city students in second through fifth grade. Not an easy task!

Instead of selecting one of my suggestions for their skit ("Jack and the Beanstalk" and "Little Red Riding Hood," among others), Latisha's group chose to fracture and reconstruct "The Gingerbread Man." I was a bit skeptical at first, because I did not know the story nor did half of the group planning to perform it. A week later I found myself surprised at their humorous and clever pantomime but even more delighted by Latisha's newfound behavior—on and off the stage. Latisha had grown up.

Needless to say, their skit was selected to be part of the production, and it delighted the kiddies and their teachers. The following year Latisha signed up for the next level of theater classes and flourished. Each week she could not wait for whatever challenge I had set up for the class in acting and directing. Then one day, out of the blue, Latisha came up to me and told me she would be out for a few weeks for an operation. I did not think much of it at first, because she was back in my class during the next session and a few after that as well. But the day came when her projected absence became a reality. During the next few months she would visit as much as possible to work with her classmates onstage or just to watch them perform in silence. On the day our new *Fractured Fairy Tales* was ready to be performed, one of my students ran backstage to inform me that Latisha was in the audience. I ran out to hug her and noticed that half of her face was altered greatly; it was sunken in and void of any movement. But her smile was ten feet wide, which helped keep me from crying right then.

During her last academic year, I saw less and less of Latisha as her visits became more about her "academic" classes. She wanted to pass her SOLs (Standards of Learning tests imposed by the state of Virginia) so that she would graduate. For Christmas, at the urging of my friend Tommy, one of my vice principals, the administrators gave her a gift of a hundred dollars instead of buying something for each other in their group. Tommy had been driving Latisha to school and back because her mother and grandmother were unable to drive. In fact, for all practical purposes, Latisha was the caregiver for them because of their extremely poor health. She was more grown up than I had ever imagined. Tommy told Latisha that he would have to call her home to let her mother know about the money she was receiving, along with a beautiful basket of goodies prepared by another vice principal, Mindy. The girl implored him not to tell them, because she would feel obliged to hand it over to her mother and grandmother. It was explained to her that the school could not give a monetary gift without letting a student's guardians know about it. But he also told her mother that the Christmas gift was for Latisha alone to do with as she pleased.

A few months later, Latisha, with only one poorly functioning eye, took eleven hours for her SOL test, reading the computer screen with a magnifying glass word by word. The teacher assigned to her had to leave at the end of the regular school day, so another teacher, my friend Jerilyn, volunteered to be the proctor for however long it might take. A few hours later she called Tommy to ask if she could order Chinese food for her young ward and herself, since it was dinnertime and Latisha still had a long time to go. Of course, permission was granted, but Latisha announced that she was going to pay for dinner. She was using part of her gift to feed her teacher.

I am happy to report that Latisha was informed that she had passed her final SOL. A happy ending? For Latisha, yes!

This brings us back to where I started: the day Latisha came in to say good-bye to her friends at school. I was not able to join them from the beginning because I was teaching my ceramics class. When I entered later, I encountered her doctors, her mother, and several teachers and counselors. She heard my voice and opened her arms wide for the biggest bear hug I have ever received. "You're here, Mr. Hanson!"

I was told that Latisha had asked her friends and teachers to stop worrying about small things and said she was sorry for any time she might have hurt us. Latisha needed to be with her other family—her school family.

Two months later, on a Monday morning, her guidance counselor asked me if I would be the guest speaker at her graduation. "Sure," I replied. "When?"

"Maybe Wednesday, maybe Friday," she replied. "We're not sure." Suddenly it all made sense to me. Latisha was going to die; she was not going to die during the summer at a "convenient time" for anyone at school who could not face up to reality, but rather, soon—very soon. A special graduation was planned for Wednesday in our auditorium with her friends and teachers, but the plans quickly changed as it became evident that she would not be able to make the trip to school. I heard nothing on Thursday, but on Friday morning we were told that the graduation was set for five o'clock that afternoon—at the hospital.

I do not know how they did it, but Latisha's counselor, secretaries, administrators, downtown bigwigs, and even the chorus were in a hospital playroom transformed by flowers, balloons, refreshments, and graduation robes for a graduation celebration. Latisha could only inaudibly mumble her gratitude. Songs were sung; speeches were made. Then, at the end, she lifted her hand and signed the symbol of love. Latisha was a high school graduate. She had accomplished her goal.

I knew that the next few days would find many guests in her hospital room, so I waited until early evening on a Tuesday to visit. When I walked in, the television was blaring with *The Jerry Springer Show*, with one of the so-called guests lifting her blouse as she screamed obscenities at her husband or boyfriend. Her exposed breasts were censored with a blurred camera covering. Latisha was oblivious to it all as she lay comatose in the hospital bed. I was too late! Drowning in devastation, I looked around helplessly. Then somehow I mustered the courage to ask her family if I might read and sing to Latisha and if it would be okay to turn off the television for just a short while. They were quite gracious and allowed me to go ahead with my planned reading.

All the time I had spent collecting records was serving a deeper purpose than I would ever have imagined. My theater training along with my education in the MGM musicals had given me the inspirational material for the best gift I could offer.

The night before, I had written a synopsis of the film version of *The Wizard of Oz*, complete with sections to insert the songs. I started to read, sing, and act out all the parts, just like I had when I was in the sixth grade. I was a child again, experiencing all the wonder of the story and score, reading and singing as if for the first time ever. That elementary school performance had come full circle. My reading and singing lasted about forty minutes. When I was finished, I kissed Latisha on the forehead and told her how much I loved her. Then I turned to the family, thanked them, and exited the room. When I reached the hospital corridor, I finally unleashed the tears I had been able to subdue during my visit—indeed during all of my encounters with Latisha in the previous year.

In school the next day Tommy told me that Latisha had passed away during the night and that I had been her last visitor. He added that earlier that morning, Latisha's brother had brought in a video of me reading and singing to Latisha and shared it with all of my administrators. At first I was mortified; it was a private moment that had been filmed without my awareness, and I felt a self-consciousness that, perhaps, I should have experienced in the sixth grade. But Tommy explained how touched the family was with my reenactment and that the rest of my administrators were moved to tears by what they had seen on the video. And then, it no longer mattered about my foolish feelings; if subliminally I had had a soothing effect on Latisha, that was good. If I hadn't, I knew that somehow I had helped her family in a very small way through an unbearable moment as Latisha faded away to a better place.

Do you suppose there is such a place, Toto? There must be.
It's not a place you can get to by a boat or a plane.
It's far, far away, behind the moon, beyond the rain…

MAY -- 2017

~~TWO WEEKS~~

DISCARD
MT PLEASANT

Made in the USA
Middletown, DE
28 March 2017